# How to Improve Self-Esteem in the African American Child

Ida Greene, Ph.D

ISBN 1-881165-15-9
Library of Congress Card Catalog Number: 96-93088
ATTENTION COLLEGES AND UNIVERSITIES, CORPORATIONS, AND PROFESSIONAL ORGANIZATIONS: Quantity discounts are available on bulk purchases of this book for educational training purposes, fund raising, or gift giving. For information contact: P. S. I. Publishers, 2910 Baily Avenue, San Diego, CA 92105, 619) 262-9951.

# My Reflections in the Present and the Future

We are at a crossroad in the Black community. Much of what I have written about in this book is the way it was when I grew up in Pensacola Florida during the 1960s. I wrote this book to help children in California learn their African American heritage of the south. Things are very different today: Young people feel disconnected from their family because the nuclear and extended family has almost disappeared. Many children are now reared by someone other than their mom and dad (grandparents, foster parents). This was unheard of when I grew up. Many children today do not know who their dad is. My dad lived in the same house with me and stayed with my mom after I was grown. Today, many children are addicted to television. We did not have a television or a telephone. And had we been able to afford both, we would not have been able to watch TV or use the phone until our homework was completed. Giving me an education was a high priority for my parents, because my mom only went to the third grade in school and she could not read or write her name.

Women, girls and the elderly were respected. Today, the Rap music calls Black women vulgar names like bitches, "hores" and Nigger. Young people use marijuana, crack, crystal, and "ecstacy". The suicide rate is on the increase and many Blacks do not want to be Black; they want good hair (long straight hair by using weaves) and many buy and wear blond wigs. There is interracial dating and marriage, with no concern about the emotional adjustment problems for children. The only positive outcome is that we have a new clean cut, intelligent, African American man, President Barack Obama, and First Lady, Michelle Obama, in the White House with their daughters Malia and Sasha.

Ida Greene, PhD, DD, MFCC, RN

# Acknowledgements

I wish to thank God for giving me the foresight to move through my, "dark nights of the soul" to complete this book. It was very difficult to move through my past emotional trauma, and remain objective. For much of the information in this book has impacted my life. I have achieved my healing in the writing of this book, and there is no longer anyone or anything to fight. I pray that the persons reading this book find it the tool they need to help our beautiful, African American children soar to great heights, and perform to their maximum capacity. My philosophy is, "each one reach one and each one teach one." We are all members of the family of mankind, when one child succeeds, we all succeed. I have used the principles in this book, in my private practice as a licensed Marriage, Family, Child Therapist, with remarkable success.

Ida Greene, PhD, DD, MFCC, RN

# Foreword

The Africans did not come to this country as free persons. They were captured as hunted animals, placed on a slave ship, restrained with rope, tied around their wrists, ankles, and bodies, and made to lie side by side, as if in a sardine can, for the journey from Africa to the Americas. After they arrived on the shores of America, they were sold as property to the highest bidder. Many landed in Virginia and were purchased by merchants in the south who needed laborers to till their crops and to pick cotton, which was the country's number one commodity at that time. Looking back at the arrival of African Americans upon the soil of the Americas, it becomes clear that they were treated inhumanely – a manner which was, then, accepted by society. African Americans were the objects of jest, viewed as childlike, comical, and stupid by whites. They lived in fear twenty-four hours a day. If they displeased their slave master, they could be beaten, tortured, or sold against their will to the highest bidder. They had no rights. They were not protected by the laws of any state or of the country as a whole.

To increase self-esteem in the African American child, one has to dispell six basic premises, these are that:

1. Our society continues to use color of skin as a measure of one's acceptance.
2. The ideal worthwhile person is blond, blue eyed, and male; the further removed one is from this standard, determines his/her not being acceptable.
3. Everything negative or bad in nature is dark or evil. Therefore, anyone with a less than white complexion will be scorned, rejected, or treated as less than equal.
4. The belief of some Europeans is that Africans, or African Americans, evolved from the ape/monkey, and were therefore wild, unruly, uncultured animals by nature with an uncontrolled sex drive.
5. Africans were considered ignorant, stupid, childlike, and with a brain smaller in size and mass than that of whites. And their unde-

veloped brain affects their ability to understand complex information.

6.  Also African Americans are the only ethnic racial group in America who came to this country as indentured slaves, and were not free people. In this role they were unable to make any decision for themselves, or for their families, until they obtained their freedom.

This book proposes that African American/Blacks are unable to resolve the color dilemma by themselves, because they were not the creators of the stereotyped, prejudicial beliefs held about them. They did not establish institutionalized racism, and likewise, they are not the perpetrators of mass media dissemination about the evils of being Black. Therefore, they are powerless to change a system that victimizes them because of their skin color. Due to years of conditioning, African Americans will need the support and aid of all conscious, loving people of the human race to change their deeply, ingrained negative self-perception. The African American cannot change white society's opinion of him or her. However, with the aid of this book, they can change their own opinion of themselves; be proud of their rich heritage and feel empowered.

The key is to have an educated, enlightened society that can help African American children to see themselves as capable, competent worthwhile people who are valuable and needed by society.

You may see the words Afro-American interchanged with African American, or Black. The word Black is generic. It may be used by persons who are mulatto or of African descent but mixed with another race. Afro-American and African American, identifies one's connection to the continent Africa. These titles all depict philosophical positions, or points of reference, used to encapsulate the pent up feelings of a people struggling to define them to become a free self-governing people who are in control of their own destiny.

# Contents

# Chapter 1

## Self-Esteem — The Essence of You

Our self-esteem is a blueprint of who you are, how you have been treated, respected, appreciated, and identified by those around you and your extended family. Your self-esteem is endless. It is the essence of who you are, not what you or others see you as. It is fragile. It can be affected by many factors, and needs continual maintenance. It reflects how you picture yourself; how you honor, respect, and value yourself. It paints a mental picture from your inner belief of who you think you can be, or what you believe you can do in life.

Your self-esteem is the vehicle you use to move through life to achieve a goal. It is the package you create to get the things you want to do, or to reach the goals you have set for yourself. Each person has a separate agenda, determined by what he or she is called to do in this lifetime. If your self-esteem is wholesome, and you feel good about yourself, you can accomplish great things. If your self-esteem is damaged, or less than what it could be, your ability to accomplish or achieve will be hampered by a negative self-concept. That negative picture creates a self-image that tells you, you are less than others, not good enough, that you cannot or will not be successful in life.

We are each marching to a different drummer. God does not repeat Himself in any two persons. Each person is unique and different. God is faceless, colorless, sexless, love, kind, understanding, powerful (Omnipotent), everywhere (Omnipresent) and all knowing (Omniscience). Therefore, who you are is God's gift to you and what you make of yourself is your gift to God.

Try to picture God as your "big" mom, dad, brother, sister; relative, friend, helper, playmate, or the many roles people play in your life. I refer to God as "It," in order not to confuse the actions or works of God with those of people.

God has magic and can do what people cannot do. God has no limitations. Because God is God, there is nothing God cannot do. God is "I AM" and all powerful, so be careful what you attach to the words "I AM," because it will occur. God is in everyone and in everything—including the storm, lightning, and thunder. This is how God purifies the earth to make it safe for us to breathe clean air. God has His own way and time to do things. You will never figure out the "whys" of life, so don't drive yourself mad or waste your time trying to do so. God is God; therefore, God has to answer to no one; God does not tell anyone what God has planned or how God will proceed.

All are created by the same God. There is one piece of cookie dough and many varieties of cookies. They range from pinkish-white, dark chocolate brown (like African Americans), brown, yellow, and olive-toned. All are related and belong to God. All things God created have a life cycle. All are born, develop, create, change, and die. Nothing is static. All is in motion, a continuous energy transformation. We are born a new each hour. This is why it does us no good to hold on to the experiences of yesterday.

Yesterday, as good as it was, is gone. It will never be repeated. Try as you may, you will never bring yesterday back. This is the way God planned it. You can get angry, curse God, shake your fist at God, God does not care. You will never be able to control God. This is the one gem of wisdom I have learned about life. You can try through trial and error to prove God is All Powerful, Everywhere, In Every Thing, or accept it.

We are one with all life and one with God. We are the daughters and sons of God. Because God loves us, it has given us an earth mother, father, and family to care for us. Some do a great job, and others do a lousy job. It matters not, because God eventually returns His children to Himself, through death.

What God does for us is determined by our relationship with Him. If you trust God, have unshakable faith in Him, love Him with all your soul, mind, and body, you will achieve greatness. However, if you rely only on your human ego, which is fallible, you will experience needless pain and suffering.

We see God through our inner eye, the imagination. So each person will see and experience God differently, according to his or her perception of God and experiences of life. If the image we have of ourselves and God is negative or distorted, it will affect how well we do in life and how we handle our life.

A negative self-image reminds us continually that we can not, or may not; measure up to the standards of society. It matters not whether this is a fact or fiction if it is believed by an individual, it will hamper greatly the contribution they make in life because he or she will be looking into a distorted mirror that reflects the message back to them, "I am different from others and I am not o.k." Depending on our self-concept/self-image, self-respect, and self-esteem, we will rise to great heights or fall into the depths of despair.

Studies have shown that girls have lower self-esteem than boys. Advertising and society's idea of how girls should look and behave are blamed for girls focusing their attention on appearance and on presenting a quiet demeanor, rather than on their abilities. Anyone can create a new image and increased self-esteem, by changing their thoughts, feelings and actions.

**ALL HUMAN BEINGS NEED THE FOLLOWING FOR SELF-ESTEEM**
1. **Security** – Self-Acceptance, a sense of belong to someone/something.
2. **Identity** – self-description given you by your family of origin.
3. **Support** – Mental, Physical and Emotional.
4. **Desire** – Dream/Vision/Goals
5. **Self-Esteem** – Internal belief about yourself and the way you experience life:
   a. **Self-Concept** – Personal and Spiritual Identity
   b. **Self-Image** – Inner picture of how you see yourself, therefore reflecting the outside you.

c. **Self-Respect** – Positive self-regard

d. **Self-Worth** – Importance to family, society, life (God)

e. **Self-Confidence** – Self-assured, comfort, inner peace

6. **Spirituality** – Your anchor, purpose for living, to contribute, make a difference.

7. **Aesthetic Appreciation** – non-human, sense of awe and majesty.

We develop a **Sense of Security** by having our birth and existence validated by someone other than ourselves. Someone, who by their words, actions, and deeds says "I am glad you were born." If you get this message from a core family member, it adds to your self-worth, self-acceptance, and helps to create a feeling of belonging, and importance.

A positive **Self-Concept** enables you to accept yourself, in spite of shortcomings or perceived deficiencies. If you acknowledge yourself as a work of fine art, a masterpiece evolving; you accept yourself as you are, with the capacity to improve, and become better. Be aware that your self-concept is not one, but two dimensional. Our self-concept is greatly influenced by what we think, how we feel and how we act. You have a Personal Self-Concept Identity and a Spiritual Self-Concept/Identity. Your self-image (inner self-picture) is formed based on the concept you have of yourself.

Your Identity is the core aspect of you. I refer to it as Self-Concept. Because of it, there are no two people alike. God created everyone different and unique. Therefore, you are special, one of a kind. You are as different from every one else in the universe as an apple is from an orange. There is no comparison between the two. God has built within each person a spiritual yardstick to which we all must grow before we die. Each lesson is equally challenging and hard for each person. We decide with God, before we come to earth the best conditions (parents, race, sex and country) to help us grow and blossom spiritually. The human experience is a refining process necessary for our soul to evolve and develop.

God allows us to decide the particulars of how we want to live our life and what we want to do or accomplish. Some of us decide to come to earth to give joy to our parents for a day, a year, seven years, or seventy years. Whatever we do with our life, it must be a masterpiece for God to behold. From God we come, and to God we return after our brief journey on earth. And since no one knows when the final hour will be to return to God, it is best that we make each day count.

You must do your best daily to be the best person you can be. Sometimes you do not get a second chance to clear up a destructive or unproductive life. It is easy to look at another person and wish you were them. Yet, you do not know the painful trials they endure as they smile. Remember, you chose this lifetime. You said yes to God and to your life circumstances. God never promised any of us that we would live a life free of hardship or challenge.

Life is an unpainted canvas. You can create as many scenes as you like. Life is a journey, not a destination. When you stop growing you slowly die. So pause if you must. Take time to enjoy the scenery and the stage production you create. For what you are is Gods' gift to you. What you make of yourself is your gift to God. When you die and leave the planet, will you leave God a masterpiece of your life experiences, or give back the heap of ashes from whence you came? Who you are is beautiful, and magnificent. You are one of a kind, a rare gem.

Your Self-Concept is the basic foundation of who you are. To be fully the person God designed, requires that you develop both your Personal and Spiritual Self-Concept. Most of us spend little time on developing our Spiritual Self-Concept. It is just as important as your Personal Self-Concept. Both aspects of your nature need to be cultivated and developed. Our other basic human needs are: Support, Desire and Self-Esteem.

**Support** – Mental, Physical, Emotional and Body. We achieve maturity and grow spiritually by working on our mental, physical, and emotional bodies. We have an inner drive to achieve, excel, and be a better person-to gain mastery over our lower nature to become the Christ within. We have been given a physical body to work through our imperfections, our negative emotions, and thoughts of self-doubt. Your goal is to seek ways to improve these three aspects of yourself. This provides the self-discipline you need to complete your primary goal of soul perfection.

**Desire** – Dreams/Goals – Believe in yourself, and know you are valuable to life. Like yourself enough to have goals. Be willing to take risks, or plan how you will live your life. The ability to dream or envision a goal is God's divine plan to inspire us to reach and stretch beyond our human limitations. Most big goals, and some little goals, require us to partner with God for their completion and success. Dreams are the longings God placed inside us to help us maintain our connection to Him. You may see me interchange the word "It" for God, to denote the impersonal nature of God. God does not have human attributes; however you may at times see humans display the attributes of God. And these attributes of God are: **Love (unconditional), Empathy, Peace, Harmony, Joy, Kindness, Compassion, Tranquility, Gentleness, Consolation, Understanding, Excellence, and Creativity**.

**Self-Esteem** – Although our self-concept has many intricate parts, our self-esteem is composed of many selves. It is your cultural upbringing, your morals and the values of your individual and cultural identities. Your self-esteem tells others how you think and feel about yourself, and your relationship to others. Webster's dictionary defines it as "A confidence and satisfaction in oneself. The California State Task Force on Self-Esteem defines it as "Appreciating my own worth, and importance, and having the character to be accountable for my self-and to act responsibly towards others." The way you act is a measure of your self-esteem. The four parts of your self-esteem are self-image, self-worth, self-respect, and self-confidence.

## KEY ELEMENTS OF YOUR CULTURAL SELF-ESTEEM

Identity/Cultural Self-Concept (morals, values)/Ethnic Pride sense of belonging→ Cultural Self-Image→ Spiritual Self-Concept/ Identity→ Self-Esteem = a) Self-Concept/Identity, b) Self-Image, c) Self-Respect, d) Self-Worth, e) Self-Confidence,

1. **Self-Concept-Cultural/Personal Identity,** formed by the mores, values of elders.

a. *Ethnic Pride* – Sense of belonging to someone or something

b. *Cultural Self-Image* – picture you create of self, based on internalized beliefs, projected outside as behavior.

c. *Spiritual Self-Concept/Identity* – Your personal *self-concept* is the active or doing part of you. Your spiritual self-concept is the *being part* of you and *God is this part.* God is experienced and exists through faith; your acceptance or belief in a Supreme Power. Or when you have a strong knowing, that what you desire God will grant, if it is wholesome, for the good of all, and does not harm you or another spiritually.

2. **Self-Esteem** – Morals and values of your individual and cultural identities.

a. *Self-Image* – The self-projected outside that you show the world. The self-image evolves continually, according to the situations and experiences you encounter. It is fragile; can be distorted, damaged, or enhanced. Your environment and the people with whom you associate determine how you see yourself. If you associate with priests, you may see yourself as a holy person. If you associate with gang bangers you may see yourself las a gang member, "Blood, Cript, or as a Skin Head".

b. *Self-Respect* – Like yourself. Have a high opinion of yourself as equal to others. If you have little or no respect for the feeling of others, it is because you have been hurt by someone. It is the nature of all human beings to be caring and kind. However, if you have been treated in an unloving, unkind manner, you will become bitter, and develop a hard exterior since you are afraid you may get

7

hurt again. One of my mothers' African sayings is "A burnt child fears fire." When unpleasant things happen to us, it makes us afraid to trust-for we fear the same thing will happen again. You must respect yourself enough to want to behave, and want to get along with others. If you are/were in trouble a lot at home, or school, the only image people will have is the bad image you have shown. You can create a new image any time you desire. However, it will require you to change. Most people are too lazy or fear change so they remain the same. We can become comfortable with a bad self-image, self- concept, or a good self-image/concept.

c. *Self-Worth* – Everyone is worthy to be alive. You are worthy to be alive or God would not have created you. If you don't feel worthy, it may be that you see yourself from a distorted negative view that needs updating. No one is all bad. To increase your self-worth, find positive traits or characteristics that set you apart from others. Ask an elderly person, or anyone who has an unbiased opinion, how they see you. We all do things sometime that makes us feel ashamed. However, we can ask God to forgive us and avoid the behavior, of which we feel ashamed.

d. *Self-Confidence* – Courage, self-assured without fear, willing to take risks. There are five types of persons that tend to destroy your confidence (belief in self). They are **Bullies, Manipulators, Braggers, Critics, and Intimidators**.

**Bullies** are insecure people. They build their confidence by reducing the confidence of others. They like to make others feel they are inferior to them. They seek people who are unsure of themselves, it makes them seem big.

*The solution to the Bully is to:* Stop comparing yourself with others.

**The Manipulator** gets pleasure from having more, or being more than other people. They exaggerate and pretend they have more than they have. Remember to only share with them non-personal information.

These people thrive on making others believe they are better than others. These people manipulate your feelings by having you feel sorry for them, and then they take advantage of your kindness.

***The solution to the manipulator is to:*** Try to limit your time with these people, especially while you are building your self-confidence.

**Braggers** – Control others through emotional tactics, intended to embarrass or frustrate others. They avoid taking responsibility for anything. It is always your fault when things do not work out as planned, not theirs. They disapprove of others to make themselves look good.

***The solution to the bragger is to:*** Not waste your time arguing with them; they will never admit to being wrong. They will always be right.

**The Critic** – Everything you do is wrong with this person. They find fault with everything. They dwell on a subject until you are aggravated, angry, or make you believe you can't do something. If you let it, their negative outlook will block your performance, stifle your growth and destroy your belief in yourself.

***The solution to the critic is to:*** Not to try and please. They build themselves up by tearing others down. Pay little attention to what they say. They will never approve of you.

**The Intimidator** – Feels superior to others. They are on a power trip. Their words and actions are intended to threaten and force you to agree with them or do what they desire. When you are intimidated you feel insecure, threatened, or powerless. You accept the other person's position of power over you, give up your opinions and accept theirs. And through force, or threat, they assume control.

***The solution to the intimidator is to:*** Learn to limit their power and control over you.

### YOUR CULTURAL SELF-ESTEEM

Your self-esteem tells how you feel about yourself. The purpose of life and growing in relationships is to refine your behavior, learn more about yourself and become a better person.

**Factors that affect our self-confidence are:**

    a. Shame (exclusion)

b. Over protection/concern

c. Hurtful words (hostility/blame)

d. Disapproval

e. Low expectations (little or no trust)

f. Ridicule

g. Fear

## SELF-CONFIDENCE

**To have self-confidence you need a "TAB"**

1. **T**hink Confident – With a "Can Do" Attitude
   a. Think "I can do it."
   b. Say to yourself "I can handle this."

2. **A**ct Confident
   a. Hold your head up
   b. Keep your shoulders back
   c. Sit tall in your seat
   d. Stand erect, with good posture

3. **B**e Confident
   a. Trust your divine (God) self to show you the way
   b. Accept excellence as a way of life – Excellence has no fear of observation.

To increase your self-confidence, write down the things you do well, or have been told you do well. Your self-esteem tells others how you feel about yourself. The purpose of life and growing through relationships is, to refine your behavior, and learn more about yourself, so you become a better person. And your self-esteem is the vehicle you use. The self-esteem can be likened to a car. It will take you where you direct it, based on your level of self-worth, self-appreciation and self-image. Your self-esteem is the vehicle you use as you travel through life. Depending upon your attitude, you will soar to great heights, or fall to the depths of despair. It determines your altitude and how much success you will achieve. You choose your attitude each day, and it is either positive or negative. You can create in your mind a glass half full or a half empty glass. Someone once said; when life gives you lemons, make lemonade. I constantly remind myself what the bible says; that the rain falls on the just and unjust alike. So if you are drinking lemonade today, just remember that you may have your lemon experiences later in life.

Know that sometimes you will smile to keep from crying, and you will sometimes smile outwardly while you cry inwardly. Sometimes, the best that you can do is pray and have faith that God will be with you as you go through your valleys of life. Life is full of valleys. So you must not despair as you grow through them. Dr. Robert Schuller talks about peak to peak experiences. Keep your attention on the peak (exalted and wonderful) experiences of life and you will hardly notice the valleys of your life.

**Persons with a high self-esteem know they have a *right to* the following things...**
Place a check mark by the ones you know you deserve.

- [ ] 1. Respect
- [ ] 2. Dignity
- [ ] 3. Esteem (to be esteemed)
- [ ] 4. Be appreciated
- [ ] 5. Empathy (to feel as another feels)
- [ ] 6. Shared sentiments
- [ ] 7. Be addressed with kind words
- [ ] 8. Be given accurate information
- [ ] 9. Be open; have two-way communication
- [ ] 10. For people to give them their full attention
- [ ] 11. Be cared for
- [ ] 12. Feel a sense of equality

An additional thing all people need is a sense of the divine or spirituality.

**Spirituality** – Our spiritual connection to a Supreme Being gives us a sense of being part of a larger group, the family of mankind. This acknowledges our relationship to all humanity. If you get a sense of your connection to the family of mankind you can travel around the world, and feel assured you would receive kindness from others. Spiritually we are all related. Our true parents are our heavenly Father/Mother not our earthly mother and father. Our true country is the Kingdom of Heaven.

**Aesthetic Appreciation** allows you to connect with the non- human world of nature, the ocean, waterfall, stars, sun, moon, sky, a tree; painting, statue, dramatic play, music, musical instrument, a song, a bird, and an airplane are all works of beauty. God, our Higher Power, Supreme Being, helps us see a larger view of the world, our place in it, and our connection to it. All has value, and is valuable, including you. The Vision of Enoch says this.

### God Speaks to Mankind

I speak to you.
Be still, know that I am God.

I spoke to you when you were born
Be still, know that I am God.

I spoke to you at your first sight.
Be still, know that I am God.

I spoke to you at your first word.
Be still, know that I am God.

I spoke to you at your first thought.
Be still, know that I am God.

I speak to you through the dew of the morning.
Be still, know that I am God.

I speak to you through the peace of the evening.
Be still, know that I am God.

I speak to you through the storm and the clouds
Be still, know that I am God.

I speak to you through the grass of the meadows.
Be still, know that I am God.

I speak to you through the trees of the forest.
Be still, know that I am God.

I speak to you through the valleys and the hills.
Be still, know that I am God.

I speak to you through the Holy Mountains.
Be still, know that I am God.

I speak to you through the rain and the snow.
Be still, know that I am God.

I speak to you through the waves of the sea.
Be still, know that I am God.

I speak to you through the splendor of the sun.
Be still, know that I am God.

I speak to you through the brilliant stars.
Be still, know that I am God.

I speak to you when you are alone.
Be still, know that I am God.

THE ESSENE GOSPEL OF PEACE – BOOK TWO

## Chapter 2

## The Beginning of You —
## the Building Blocks of Self-Concept

Your self-identity is beautiful, and magnificent. It is one of a kind, it is a rare gem. It is the basic foundation of you. There are many things that affect the person we are, and the person (face) we present to the world. Remember, you were chosen to live this lifetime. You said yes to God and to life. Always remember that you are a child of God. In Romans 8:16-17, It states "The Spirit itself bears witness, that we are the children of God; and if children, then heirs of God, and joint-heirs with Christ." You came from God and to God you return when you die. You did not come from your parents; you came through them. God is the source of all life, including yours. You have an inheritance from God of: intelligence, a perfect body, mind, perfect health, unlimited power, prosperity, joy, peace, and God's unconditional love. All of this was given to you at birth. All you need to do is to claim your birth rights, and accept the gifts that came with your royal, divine heritage as a child of God. You did not inherit disease, poverty, nervousness or bad luck. So ask yourself if you are patterning your life after your human parents, or your divine spiritual parent.

Seek to do your best daily, to be the best person you can be. Sometimes you do not get a second chance to clear up a destructive or unproductive life. It is easy to look at another person, and wish you were them. Yet you do not know the painful trials they endure as they smile. God never promises any of us we will live a life free of hardship or challenge. Your challenges take the rough edges of you, so that you sparkle like a diamond. "*I will turn all your mountains into a road, and your highways shall be raised up.*" Isaiah 49:11.

Life is an unpainted canvas and you can create as many scenes as you desire. Life is a journey, not a destination. When you stop growing you slowly die. So pause if you must, but do not give up. Take time to

15

enjoy the scenery and the stage production you create. For what you are is God's gift to you. What you make of yourself is your gift to God. When you die and leave the planet will you leave God a masterpiece of your life experiences, or will you give back the heap of ashes from which you came?

You are composed of many thoughts, feelings, beliefs, attitudes, emotions, wishes, longings, limitations, disappointments, setbacks, dreams, hopes, and aspirations. Are you aware of the many parts that make the whole of you?

## Personal Self-Concept→ (a. Expressive b. Creative) → Societal (Public) Social Self-Concept→ Spiritual/Universal Self-Concept

**Your Self-concept has three selves.**
1. **Personal Self-Concept a. *Expressive Self***, it is your ability to provide for your self, your money making ability. **b. *Creative self*** – reflects your personal growth; it may be expressed through your desire for success, and to achieve. It is your tendency to create your ideal self. It is an inner essence that is undiscovered, waiting to burst forth.
2. **Societal/Social Self** – Focuses on relationships and your interpersonal relationships
3. **Spiritual/Self-Concept** – This divine part of you makes you reach out to help others. Your self-concept is an expression of how you perceive (see) yourself. The perception of you can vary from situation to situation.

Your Personal Self-Concept creates your daily circumstances through your thoughts, beliefs and visions.
a.   Expressive self – Your money-making ability.
b.   Creative self – Your personal growth, undiscovered self-and talents.

Sometimes one's cultural values may differ from the larger societal values and cause confusion or conflict for an individual. For example, if one's cultural values say it is o.k. to steal as long as you do not get caught, while the larger societal values says stealing is never an acceptable behavior, the discrepancy can cause confusion and uncertainty as how one should behave. The way one sees them self-differs with how society sees them. Your cultural self-identity provides morals and values. It acts as a guideline for what is acceptable conduct and manners.

## YOUR PERSONAL SELF-CONCEPT

Your Personal Identity/Self-Concept is the imprint given to you by your family. Sometimes we inherit a distorted self-concept because the behavior and attitude we see displayed in our family may be acceptable there, however it may be not acceptable in society. An example of this would be to tell someone a lie or borrow someone's personal belonging without asking their permission.

Your Personal Identity/Self-Concept is the private you that may be at odds with the values and morals of your family. For example, on my fathers' side of the family (Albert Green), "The Greens' do not believe in divorce, they work things out, or place them in the hands of the Lord. I was reprimanded when I decided to divorce my husband, even though fornication is a legitimate biblical reason.

Usually your Personal Self-Concept will focus on power how much you have or can exercise. You do not have any power. You merely use the power in the universe for either good or bad. It is how you express yourself and view your relationship to God. Ask yourself if you believe there is a Supreme power that rules the earth or do you see yourself as the ultimate power in the universe? If you say yes, that places a tremendous burden on you to control everything, and little time to enjoy life. Also if you are the ultimate power you should be able to keep everyone alive forever including yourself. If you are the ultimate power, then you can decide when day will end, and nighttime begins. You also decide when it will rain, snow, thunder, whether the day will be cloudy or sunshine. Isn't it wonderful to be a child of God, so you do not have to worry about these things? Always remember that as a child of God, you are the little "I," not the "Big I." You are the image of God, the "little God," not the "Big God."

Personal Self-Concept/Identity→ Cultural Self-Concept (values)
Ethnic Pride creates belonging→ Self-Image→ Self-Esteem

## Your Cultural Self-Concept

Our cultural self-concept/identity is formed partly from our cultural identity through the morals and values shared with us by elders and the ethnic pride we develop, all serve to create a sense of belonging. From this sense of belonging we form our self-image. Since we see from the inside out, we may not always have an accurate picture of who we are. Also if any of the parts that come together to formulate our self-image are distorted, our self-image will likewise be distorted. An example of a distorted self-image is someone who weighs ninety pounds but their mental picture sees a fat person. To change your self-image it will require that you change your self-concept to improve your self-image. And to improve your self-esteem requires you to work to improve your self-concept/identity (cultural identity, ethnic pride), and self-image.

## Key elements of your cultural self-identity

A. **Cultural Identity/Self-Concept**→ (morals, values) →

B. **Ethnic Pride** creates a sense of belonging→

C. **Self-Image**→

D. **Self-Esteem**

    1. Self-Worth,

    2. Self-Respect,

    3. Self-Confidence

One's identity as a member of a culture or a clan helps formulate your self-concept. It is a point of reference about who one is and where they came from. Most cultures have a set of values of acceptable or appropriate behaviors one is expected to display. Sometime one's cultural values may differ from the larger societal values causing confusion or conflict for an individual. For example if one's cultural values say it is o.k. to steal as long as you do not get caught, and the larger societal values say stealing is never an acceptable behavior, the child will experience confusion and be uncertain how to behave. Then the way one sees/perceives themself is at odds with how society sees them. Your self-perception can vary from situation to situation. A. Cultural Self-Concept/Identity – Morals, values of acceptable behaviors:

**Cultural Self-Concept/Identity** – Your cultural self-identity provides morals and values and acts as a guideline for what are acceptable behaviors of conduct and manners. It is your identity as a member of a culture, or clan. It helps to formulate the self-concept. It is a point of reference about who one is, and where one comes from. Most cultures have a set of values of acceptable or appropriate behaviors one is expected to display. Examples are:

A. Cultural values of *acceptable behaviors*
1. Not speaking while another is speaking
2. Asking before you touch the property of another
3. Saying – "please and thank you."

B. Cultural values of *unacceptable behaviors* write others below:
1. Stealing – taking from others without their permission.
2. Dishonesty-
3.

**1. Societal/Social Self-Concept** – focuses on your personal, and interpersonal relationships. The American culture does not have a Societal Self-Concept. It is the nature of your social self-to attach itself to those it identifies as societal family. Society has no moral or ethical guidelines for non Christian, non secular persons to follow. There is no vehicle to teach or provide moral training if anyone is interested in getting it.

**2. Societal (Public) Self-Concept** is reflected through your People Skills. It is your ability to interact effectively with others. The part of you that does what is socially acceptable. Your school and work cultures reflect this self. If you are not accepted as a part of the culture where

19

you are, you will experience confusion, feel detached, disorganized, and have a sense of uneasiness until you know why you are rejected. Once you know the reason/s for your non-acceptance, you can decide if you can handle the social isolation, or do something about it.

You have several options: you can become a rebel, recluse, start your own elite group, or pretend it doesn't matter. Meanwhile, your self-image, self-esteem, and self-confidence decay as a result of the dual messages you are sending to it: "I'm o.k. /I'm not o.k. /Am I really o.k.?"

The government was never designed to teach morality. It is not a preventative institution. It deals strictly with the law. It punishes its members after they break the law. It does not teach moral laws, the churches do that. Since the two entities can not co-mingle, society has to build more jails to punish people for their ignorance of moral laws or morality.

However due to the separation of state between church and government, the American society has become more government, and little or no church. The church is the institution that provides moral training; however our society does not respect churches as in the past. The Bible for many Americans has become sports, entertainment activities, television, and Hollywood.

Many people do not know that the spiritual laws of the Ten Commandments say "Thou shalt not kill," and "Thou shalt not steal." Society does not teach this, so people continue to steal and kill. Many people do not know right conduct from wrong conduct. Often when they discover this they are older than age seven, when most behavior patterns are firmly established. We always behave according to our self-concept, whether it is moral or amoral.

Societal values are general and non binding. Cultural Assimilation – means we can choose to be a part of a society, or we can isolate ourselves and be uninvolved with the people around us. Cultural Integration means blending into societal fabric. All cultures have behavioral do's and do not's to guide its citizens. The American culture is judeo Christian and follows the Ten Commandments in the Bible as a guide for how we should behave towards each other. Our cultural guidelines for living and getting along with each other use the principles in the Ten Commandments given to Moses by God. You will probably find some of your cultural do's and don'ts in the Ten Commandments, even though you may not be Judeo Christian. The general principles set forth in the Ten Commandments are:

## TEN COMMANDMENTS

1. Thou shall have no other Gods before me. You shall love the Lord your God with all your mind, body and soul.
2. Thou shall love thy neighbor as thy self.
3. Thou shall make no graven (carved, sculptured) image of anything that is above the earth or below the sea. No idolatry. Idolatry includes the worship of anything, as if it were independent from God.
4. Thou shall not steal. No theft.
5. Thou shall not kill. No murder.
6. Thou shall honor thy mother and thy father. (Includes persons who take the place of an inadequate mom or dad).
7. Thou shall not use the name of the Lord in vain. (I swear to God, God ....) No blasphemy of God's name.
8. Thou shall not commit adultery. (Take things that belong to your neighbor, be it a toy, car, girl friend/wife, boyfriend/husband). No adultery, incest or living together before marriage.
9. Thou shall not bear false witness against thy neighbor. (Tell a lie) Always tell the truth even if it gets you in trouble. It is better to be in trouble with people than with God, by breaking one of these Commandments.
10. Remember the Sabbath day to keep it holy. (Set aside one day to honor God)

The American culture is Judeo-Christian and follows the Ten Commandments in the Bible; however, due to the separation of state between church and government, the American society has become more government and little or no church. The church is the institution that provides moral training; however our society does not respect churches as it did in the past.

**3. Spiritual Self-Concept** – Your Spiritual Identity is the core aspect of you. I refer to it as the self-concept. There are no two people alike. God created everyone different and unique. Therefore you are special. There is no one in the world that possesses all of your character traits. We decide the particulars of how we want to live our life and what we want to do or accomplish. Someone may choose to come to earth as a child to give joy to the parents for a day, a year, seven years or 70 years.

There is a part of us that connects to a Supreme Deity, I refer to as God. We show our divinity when we are kind, considerate, tolerant, compassionate, and understanding. All of these are traits of God. God has implanted Himself within our heart, so that He can minister to us and through us to our earth brothers and sisters. However we must open our mind and heart, so we are able to receive the divine inspiration and guidance God wishes us to receive. We can all be earth angels by loving our fellow humans and behaving in a divine and angelic manner. We do this through unconditional love for each other and forgiving the offenses of others seventy times seventy.

In the Old Testament, the orthodox Hebrews had over 600 laws to follow daily to live a Godly life. In the New Testament, the laws have been reduced to two, "loving God and loving your neighbor as yourself". When you love God and see yourself as a child of God it is easy to love yourself without arrogance. When you can love yourself without arrogance or self-hatred it will be easy to extend the feeling to your neighbor. For the answer to every problem you will encounter is **Love**. Love the problems you now encounter for they bring you new wisdom, growth, and maturity.

Love the solution or answer you receive, for it holds blessing beyond your wildest imagination. If you see a problem or situation from a negative perspective it will be negative. If you change your view, where you now see a problem to a different one, you will feel different about yourself and your relationship to the situation you now see as a problem.

It is important to understand your relationship to God. You are a child of God; therefore whatever your needs God will supply. You were given an earth (human) mother and father, to care for you, and look after your needs. Sometimes they turn out to not be the best. If that happened to you, take the matter to God and "It" will find you a substitute. This substitute mother or father may be a neighbor, or family member who acts like a mom/dad or any other person God chooses. The secret is that you must not get mad and brood because your parents are not the way you would like them. Speak to God in private, through your prayers, and ask for what you want. God is not like humans, so the answer to your prayers may be delayed, while God searches for the perfect solution. This is where your faith and belief that God has heard your prayer becomes critical. God hears your prayers, and answers in *God's own time*, not your time. Your time may not produce the best outcome. Always remember that God can see further up the road through His spiritual eyes than you can see with your limited human eyes. And always remember that God will answer your prayers if what you're asking for is in His Will for you, not your will for yourself.

Remember what the Bible says about God. God is a spirit, "they that worship him, must worship him (It) in spirit and in truth." (God is sexless and colorless). You worship God in truth when you know the truth about yourself. You were created in the image and likeness of God. Therefore you are perfect as you are. You may have a few personality, or ego, rough edges that need to be smoothed out. However that does not mean you are worthless, or no good. A diamond is perfect, but its brilliance is greater after you smooth off its rough edges. Likewise, you are a work of creative art in progress.

You are perfect as a human being; however you need to be refined for your inner brilliance to show. All human beings agree to come to earth to have a human experience to become flawless as their Mother, Father, and God in heaven. It is sad we do not remember we agreed and wanted to come to earth. It was our choice to have a human experience. We asked God if we could be born of human parents, to learn certain lessons or develop a particularly weak character trait or traits. God is not like your earth mom or dad, who is finite and dies. God is birth less and deathless. I must admit in my quiet discussions with God, I have said I did not know what I was getting into when I asked to be born. I did not know the lessons I needed to learn would be so painful. There have been times when I said I was ready to make my transition and come back for another trial. And in the next breath say, God I didn't mean that. What I really meant is "God would you lighten my load a little bit." I need to rest for a short time, then I will be ready for whatever challenges you send my way. I have decided to master all the lessons I need to learn and work through whatever shortcomings I have. I do not want to repeat this earth experience.

I used to feel as if I were being singled out for trials and tribulation, but then I reread the Bible and it said "the sun shines on the just and unjust alike." Life is what we make it. When things are progressing as we like, the world is a great place to be, and when we are going through our growth phase, we wish we were not alive. We created our world by the thoughts we think. If you keep your mind on highly spiritual, uplifting thoughts, the valley will not seem as dark the next time you pass through it. Because we create our world daily, our self-concept and self-image changes daily. *On the next page draw a picture of how you see yourself*. Next to that picture draw how you would like to look or be your ideal self.

## YOUR SELF-PERCEPTION

1. List below four traits or qualities you would most like to have. Then state what you can do to become this person.

a. ..................................................................

b. ..................................................................

c. ..................................................................

d. ..................................................................

2. Finish this sentence – **I am special because**…

a. ...............................................................................

b. ...............................................................................

c. ...............................................................................


*The spirit of God has made me, and the breathe of the Almighty gives me life*
— JOB 33:4

*You are precious in my sight, and I love you*
— ISAIAH 43:4


ON ACHIEVEMENT
*If you can imagine it, you can achieve it*
*If you can dream it, you can become it*
— KRISTONE


**Your Cultural Self-Image** – It is an inner picture of how you see yourself as reflected in behavior. Our culture gives us information about our ancestors, family members who lived before us. Our culture helps us create a point of reference as the beginning of our self.

Our self-concept/identity is formed partly from our cultural identity through the morals and values shared with us by elders. And the ethnic pride we develop creates a sense of belonging. From this belonging we form our self-image.


**Ethnic Pride** – is an important element provided by one's cultural group. It gives one a sense of belonging and acts as a point of reference.

It gives distinction, or can be a source of embarrassment and disgrace. This is especially true if the family member is a noted gang/drug leader, or a relative of Dr. Martin Luther King. And there are family celebrations such as yearly family reunions, or a special community event, in the African American community called Kwanzaa. *Some cultural values or unacceptable behaviors for southern African Americans*:

1. Stealing – taking from others without their permission.
2. Dishonesty – telling an untruth (lie)
3. Lack of respect for elders (their wisdom and advice sought)
4. To not argue (talk back to adults)

Write other cultural values of unacceptable behavior:
1.
2.
3.

List some ethnic values of your family/clan below
1.
2.

A. Write below, the values your family or culture of origin feels is acceptable:

...................................................................

...................................................................

**On Encouragement**
*Within our reach lies every path we ever dream of taking.*
*Within our power lies every step we dream of making.*
*Within our range lies every joy we dream of seeing...*
*Within ourselves lies everything we ever dream of being.*
– AMANDA BRADLEY

Our culture provides an identity for us of how those who look like us began. It gives us a map to follow, and shows us how to begin. When the child is young, it seeks a point of reference as the beginning of self: Where did I come from? To whom do I belong? How did I get to earth? Are there other people who look like me? Our cultural ethnic identity answers this question. In the space below fill in the blanks with the appropriate information about your family tree.

**My name is** ................................. SexM/F...............

My birth date ................................. Birth weight .........

My birth place................................. Time of birth ......

Number of brothers, and names ......................................

.................................................................

Number of sisters, and names ......................................

.................................................................

.................................................................

My favorite food/s ................................................

My favorite colors ................................................

My favorite animal/pet ............................................

**Father's name** ............................................................

His birth date ...................................Birth weight .........

Birth place ......................................Time of birth .........

**Things I remember my father/male guardian saying to me**

.......................................................................

.......................................................................

.......................................................................

**Mother's name** (married)  ...........................................

Maiden name..........................................................

Birth date  ................................... Birth weight .........

Birth place ......................................Time of birth .........

**Things I remember my mother/guardian saying to me**

.......................................................................

.......................................................................

.......................................................................

## My Father's Mother

**Grandmother's name** ..................................................

Birth date ...................................Birth weight .........

Birth place ...................................Time of birth .........

Things I remember her saying to me ...............................

..........................................................................

..........................................................................

..........................................................................


## My Father's Father

**Grandfather's name** ..................................................

Birth date ................................... Birth weight .........

Birth place ...................................Time of birth .........

Things I remember him saying to me ...............................

..........................................................................

..........................................................................

..........................................................................

## My Mother's Mother

**Grandmother's name** ....................................................

Birth date .................................... Birth weight .........

Birth place .................................... Time of birth .........

Things I remember her saying to me ...............................

........................................................................

........................................................................

........................................................................


## My Mother's Father

**Grandfather's name** ....................................................

Birth date .................................... Birth weight .........

Birth place .................................... Time of birth .........

Things I remember him saying to me ...............................

........................................................................

........................................................................

........................................................................

Write any thoughts or feelings you have about your core family members. Which person has contributed positively to your self-esteem and self-confidence? What did they do?

We see from the inside out, so we may not always have an accurate picture of who we are. If any part that formulates our self-image is distorted, our self-image will be distorted. An example of a distorted self-image is someone who weighs ninety pounds, but whose inner mental picture sees a fat person. To change a distorted self-image will require you to change your self-concept. Thus to improve your self-esteem requires you to improve your self-concept/identity, cultural identity, ethnic pride, and self-image. There are key elements of your self-esteem that are essential for good emotional maturity. They are self-respect, self-worth, and self-confidence. Your self-image is based on your self-concept.

The definition of a person with a high self-esteem is one who has a positive attitude along with a feeling of "I am a valuable person, I am capable, and I can do it." Did you ever think about the concept (mental image) you hold of yourself? It is an inner mental picture. Stop what you are doing now, and draw your self-concept. *Draw it with your non-dominant hand in the space below* (your left hand if you are right handed).

## FACTORS THAT SHAPE OUR SELF-IDENTITY/SELF-ESTEEM

There are many things that affect the person we are, and the person (face) we present to the world. Are you aware that there are many parts that make the whole of you? You are composed of many thoughts, feelings, beliefs, attitudes, emotions, wishes, longings, limitations, disappointments, setbacks, dreams, hopes, and aspirations.

**As you go through this list, place a (+) or (-) by any category that evokes a positive or negative reaction in you, and state why underneath each section.**

1. Parental readiness and acceptance

2. Sex of child

3. Cultural concept of beauty, what it means to be beautiful.

4. Physical and emotional health of mother

5. Physical health of infant

6. Cultural customs, folklore, beliefs, ethnic identity and pride

7. Behavior expectation-what you need to do/say to be a    family member

8. No support system for bonding (grand parent, aunt, uncle). Do you have a support system for bonding?

A. Do you have a substitute for an ineffective family member/s?  For example, play mom (someone you ask to play the role of your mom, because she is unable, due to alcohol or drugs). Who is this person? Whose roles are they taking? Your dad or mom?

B. Do you like your extended family members? (Aunts, uncles, cousins). Why?

C. Are there any family members you dislike? Why?


Our culture gives us information about our ancestors, family members who lived in Africa and were brought to America as slaves. Although Africans were slaves when they arrived in America, they were considered royalty in Africa, a King, Queen, Prince, and Princess.

**Finish this sentence**: I am royalty because....

A. ...................................................................

...................................................................

B. ...................................................................

...................................................................

C. ...................................................................

...................................................................

I am good at doing the following:

1. .............................

2. .............................

3. .............................

### MORE WITHIN

*An acorn is more than just an acorn,*
*Within it is a giant oak*
*A caterpillar is more than just a caterpillar;*
*Within it is a brilliant butterfly.*
*An egg is more than just an egg;*
*Within it is a beautiful bird.*
*A thought is more than just a thought;*
*Within it is a generous deed.*
*A dream is more than just a dream;*
*Within it is a joyous reality.*
*An infant is more than just a infant;*
*Within it is a triumphant adult.*
*Unfinished things are more than human eyes can see,*
*And "mortals are more than we appear to be!"*
— WILLIAM ARTHUR WARD (deceased 1995)

**Self-Image** – We see from the inside out, so we may not always have an accurate picture of who we are. If any part that formulates your self-image is distorted, your self-image will be distorted. To change a distorted self-image, you will need to change your self-concept. And to improve your self-esteem it will require you to improve your self-concept/identity, cultural identity, ethnic pride, and self-image. These are key elements of your self-esteem that is essential for emotional maturity.

Write below three attitudes or behaviors you dislike about yourself. Put a check mark by the ones you would most like to change. Also state three things you can do to change the trait.

1. ...........................

2. ...........................

3. ...........................

I am at ease with myself.

I honor myself rightly so I am not overly confident, nor honor myself too little.

I am an expression of the Divine, therefore I am O.K.

I am a part of the Divine principle of the universe.

I am whole, perfect, and complete just as I am.

I accept that to be perfect means I can become better, improve, and make corrections in my personality, relationships and lifestyle.

I accept that all perfect things can become better, including me.

I accept myself at my emotional, mental, spiritual level of learning.

I accept that as I grow and evolve, I evolve into a better person with a new concept of myself and others.

It is O.K. for me to give and receive praise.

I let it be O.K. for me to give support and be supported.

– AUTHOR UNKNOWN (Modified and adapted by Ida Greene)


## FACTORS THAT LOWER OUR SELF-ESTEEM

- Disrespectful behavior, self-limiting beliefs, negative thoughts. Can you think of a time when this happened to you?

- Ridicule/embarrassment, shame, confusion, or hurtful words that make one feel badly.
- Inadequate support system for bonding, ineffective family member/s.
- Tendency to be, does, or acts to gain acceptance or belong.
- Both praise and punishment act as a positive or negative reinforcement and has the ability to influence your behavior.
- Difference: Be treated differently from others in your family, or group.
1. Write about self-limiting beliefs, thoughts or behaviors you see in yourself.

..................................................

..................................................

..................................................

A. Where did you hear these statements?

..................................................

B. Write name of person who said this, by the remark, for example:
   *"This is hard " (a belief you heard)* ......**John Doe**
   a. I can't do this (a behavior) ..................................
   b. This is too much for me to do (thought)......................
   c. I don't like this/I hate doing this.............................
   d. I don't like her-him/I hate him/her ........................
   d. I will never finish/get this done ..............................
   f. This is boring, no fun and stupid..............................

C. Say the above statements aloud. Do you feel energized or tired?

   1. How much feeling do you have to *be*, or *act out* the above?

D. Listed below are some examples of positive beliefs/thoughts, attitudes, and behaviors:
   a. This is easy
   b. I can do this
   c. This is fun
   d. I am good at this
   e. I am smart
   f. Learning to do something new is fun

E. Say the above statements aloud. Do they make you feel *good* or
   *bad*?

1. Write down your positive beliefs, thoughts and behaviors below:

F. Now it is your turn, write your positive, self-enhancing statements, and say them aloud to yourself.

a. I am intelligent
b. I figured "it out," I am smart.
c.
d.

G. Which category of beliefs above has affected your self-esteem? Write your answer below:

H. Has this influenced your home life or school performance? How?

1. What did you learn about yourself from the above exercises?

2. Did you discover anything new about you, new learning or ideas?

## TODAY

*This is the beginning of a new day.*
*God has given me this day to use as I will.*
*I can waste it. or use it for good.*
*But what I do today is important because*
*I am exchanging a day of my life for it.*
*When tomorrow comes,*
*This day will be gone forever.*
*Leaving in its place*
*Something that I have traded for it.*
*Good and not evil,*
*Success and not failure,*
*In order that I shall not regret*
*The price that I have paid for it.*

*—*KRISTONE

## SELF ESTEEM ASSESSMENT

1. Who am I? I am....

2. Are you like your **mom** or **dad**? Is that good or bad?

3. What makes you special/unique from others in your family or class?

4. What are your talents or gifts (things you do with ease that takes effort for others)?

5.  What are your strengths and your weaknesses?

6.  What makes your ancestry (family tree) special?

7.  Ask yourself, "How do I acknowledge myself without putting others down, who looks or acts different from me?"

8.  What can you do to communicate with others if you are shy or easily embarrassed?

9.  Do you make friends easily with strangers? If your answers is no, rethink, what can you do to overcome this handicap?

10. How do you let the opposite sex know that you want to be their friend?

11. How much money will you make in 20 yrs?

12. How do you plan to get it?

## RISK

*To laugh is to risk appearing a fool.*

*To weep is to risk appearing sentimental.*

*To reach out for another is to risk involvement.*

*To expose feelings is to risk exposing your true self.*

*To place your ideas, your dreams before a crowd*
*    is to risk their loss.*

*To love is to risk not being loved in return.*

*To live is to risk dying.*

*To hope is to risk despair.*

*To try is to risk failure.*

*But risks must be taken, because the greatest hazard*
*    in life is to risk nothing.*

*The person who risks nothing, does nothing, has nothing,*
*    is nothing*

*They may avoid suffering and sorrow, But they*
*    cannot learn, feel, change, grow, love, or live.*

*Chained by their certitudes, they are a slave,*
*    they have forfeited their freedom.*

*Only a person who risks is free.*

– ANON


## POSITIVE SELF-REGARD AFFIRMATIONS

*I like me.*

*I am wise.*

*I deserve to be alive.*

*I am worthy.*

*I am worthy of recognition.*

*I accept myself, just as I am.*

*I accept my skin color, for it is beautiful.*

*I am proud to be a (n)* .....................................

– IDA GREENE

**Things you can do to help yourself and your family**

- Be supportive of your parents or guardians, and be willing to spend time with, and take responsibility for your siblings.

- Be a team player. Be a real family member. Family members help each other and help out around the house.

- Help out around the house; choose two chores you will be responsible to do without money from your parents.

- Don't be a freeloader, and expect your family and friends to always give to you. Give as well as receive.

- Do not stand with your hands out, always waiting to get or receive. There is great joy in giving with no expectation to receive or be compensated. This is angelic work. It is compensated divinely.

- Model positive behavior to your friends and younger children. Do not smoke, drink, or use drugs.

- Study your school work every night- even if no one tells you to. It is your brain you need to feed. Care enough about yourself to feed your mind with wholesome thoughts and ideas.

- Limit your television viewing time to no more than **one hour a night on school nights**. *Avoid watching movies with violence, sex, or horror before you go to sleep at night.* Whatever activity you do before going to sleep will make a positive imprint in your brain.

- Stay in school and do well. Plan for college or a profession

- Encourage your friends to stay in school and do well.
- Volunteer and do community service by helping at a senior center, church, or neighborhood activities.

- Keep yourself physically fit. Exercise, eat fruits, and vegetables, and encourage your friends to do the same.

- Know how to get help for friends who get in trouble. Know where alcohol and drug treatment, counseling, and health services are located within your community.

## ENHANCE SELF-ESTEEM TO *LIGHT THE FIRE WITHIN YOU*™

Through our desires and goals we become motivated to change our circumstances

**Drive to Excel→ Goal Directness → Energy/Vitality → Enthusiasm → Light Aliveness → (Joy, Happiness, Love) = FIRE**
**Desire → Drive → Enthusiasm → Energy → Light/Aliveness = Good Feelings about Self**

### THINGS THAT BLOCK GOOD FEELINGS ABOUT YOURSELF

**Confidence blockers** are those feelings and situations where your confidence melts away and you wish you were someone else.

**Confidence blockers** are the uncertainties and insecurities we all feel in different areas of our lives, the fear of "not measuring up," and fears of not being whom and what we'd like to be.

When does your confidence fizzle? What situations or feelings send your confidence level falling?

1. **Being criticized?**
2. **Feeling out of place?**
3. **Personal rejection?**
4. **Feeling poor?**

Overcoming **confidence blockers** requires positive actions that eliminate, or offset your loss of confidence caused by negative responses and uncomfortable situations.

The secret for overcoming **confidence blockers** lies in your ability to accept change — your ability to learn new skills, adopt new attitudes and seek new information.

The specific actions necessary to overcome your **confidence blockers** depend on you or the situation. However, all actions and efforts are focused on finding ways to overcome the confidence drain so you learn to feel better about yourself. Start today to change, *the only thing you have to lose is feeling lousy*.

Do any of these **confidence blockers** really get you down? Add your own to the list. Remember, identifying the **confidence blockers** is the first step toward getting rid of them.

### Confidence blockers

**Criticizing** yourself or others.

**Complaining** about yourself, your conditions, or others.

**Condemning** yourself or others, have a strong bias or prejudice for.

Are you guilty of *saying* or *doing* any of the above?
Write comments below:

.................................................................................

.................................................................................

.................................................................................

.................................................................................

## SOME WAYS TO IMPROVE YOUR SELF-ESTEEM

a.   Give thanks to God for air you breathe and food you eat.

b.   Say to yourself-"Yes, I can do this," or "Let me give it a try."

c.   Forgive yourself, parents, or friends for unknown mistakes.

d.   Give a smile to everyone you meet, including yourself.

e.   Keep peace in your heart, and think peaceful thoughts.

f.   Love God, humanity and yourself in that order.

g.   Never make another person your God.

h.   Never compare yourself to anyone, for there will always be persons greater, or lesser than you.

| The following is true about me | The following is not true about me |
|---|---|
| 1 | 1 |
| 2 | 2 |
| 3 | 3 |
| 4 | 4 |
| 5 | 5 |
| 6 | 6 |

*Shoot for the Moon, Even if you Miss You Will Land Among the Stars!*

— ANON

## LIFE MIRRORS OUR BELIEF

What are your beliefs about yourself? Write your answers below:

## MY SELF-PERCEPTION

Think of words that describe you. Use words that tell others something about you. Example -The word friendly, pretty, etc. Your #1 word will tell how you best feel about yourself, and your #2 word next best and so forth.

1. ................................................................................

2. ................................................................................

3. ................................................................................

4. ................................................................................

5. ................................................................................

## EXERCISES TO INCREASE YOUR SELF-WORTH

These are exercises to empower yourself and increase self-worth

1. Write **words** you feel *best describe you*.

2. What **words** would others use to describe you? *Why*?

3. Are you excited daily about getting up for school? *Why*?

4. Why were you created?

   To do **what**?

   To be **whom** ?

   To do it **when**?

   To be **where**?

   For **whom**?

5. What kind of work will you do as an adult to earn money?

6. If you could live any place in the **U.S. or the World** where would it be?

7.  If you could do what you wanted, what would you **be**?

    If you could have **what you wanted**, What would it be?

    What would you do?

8.  What do you think **successful people do** to become successful?

9.  How much education do you want?

    Do you feel this will occur?

10. Will you go to college?
    Where?

    Will you graduate from college?

11. What is your favorite food/s?

12. Your Favorite car?

What is your idea of fun?

Do you have enough happy times in your life? Your thoughts control your life. And the questions you ask yourself determine your happiness. **Write five thoughts you are saying to yourself now.** Are they happy or unhappy memories?

*It was once said: If you think education is expensive — try the cost of ignorance!*
– AUTHOR UNKNOWN

*Misery is the shadow we see between ourselves and the light of the universe (God). So watch what you think and what you say.*

### Self-Esteem, the Essence of You

1. The key elements that negatively affect your self-esteem are:

**Culture➔ Identity➔ Ethnic Pride➔Acculturation
Assimilation➔ Ridicule/Embarrassment➔ Shame➔
Confusion ➔ Feelings of Less Than**

   A. Which category/ies has had a negative effect on the development of your self-esteem?

   B. State how this has influenced your personal life/school.

   C. What beliefs do you hold, that block your personal relationship, or spiritual growth?

To *Light the Fire within You*™, learn how to be in control of your emotions and destructive urges. List ways you can avoid the following.

1.   Resentment

2. Jealousy

3. Hostility

4. Rage

5. Shyness – is caused by shame, embarrassment, or ridicule.

### *Light The Fire Within You*™
### Healing the shattered self-image

1. Have you forgiven your parents, childhood caretakers, or others who had power to negatively influence your life? Write their name below.

2. What negative thoughts or attitudes do you have toward your parents?

3. These are ways I can develop my capacity to care and feel positive emotions towards myself:

4. I am learning to forgive and love myself and others who mistreated me in my childhood. Write names of people you need to forgive

5. What part of your self-image needs to be changed?

6. Write any negative thoughts or attitudes you have towards your parents/caretaker.


7. Are you able to forgive your parents, yourself, God? What can you do to heal this relationship?


8. List anything that makes you feel sad, mad, anxious, or glad.
   I feel sad when I think about

   ....................................................................

   I feel mad when I think about

   ....................................................................

   I feel anxious when I think of

   ....................................................................

   I feel glad when I think about

   ....................................................................

9. What can you do to cope with feeling unloved?


   A. Also learn to forgive anyone who has mistreated you. Can you think of anyone you need to forgive?


   B. List everyone below you need to forgive. write a sentence to them. For example:
      Mom – Mom, I forgive you for not showing me loves.
      Dad – Dad, I forgive you for ignoring/criticizing me.

C. Overlay any negative feelings with positive feelings for persons listed above.

D. List things you can do to show love to yourself.

E. Sit quietly, practice sending love arrows to yourself or others who mistreated you.

6. Self-Confidence is a feeling of being self-assured or comfort with what you say or do. Can you think of an activity, or behavior you do, where you feel calm and self-assured?

A. If not, what can you do to feel at ease with yourself when you perform in the presence of others?

B. Are your expectations for yourself realistic?

7. There are no two people alike. God created everyone different. Are you angry with God that you are unique?
A. Do you tell yourself you must be perfect to be an O.K. person?

B. Do you like yourself?
Why?


Why not?


C. Is there someone you like better than yourself?
Why?


D. List below thought you have/believe about yourself.


8. Do you want a family?
a)  Can you handle this responsibility?
What will you do/how will you do this?


b)  Do you want a small or large family?

c)  Will you send them to college?


E. You will need $100 000 to feed and clothe a child to age 18, and
send them to college. Write your plans below as to why, what, when,
and how regarding a family and children.
How wiill you provide for a small family of two children?

How will you provide for a **large family**, three or more?

## Positive Self-Regard Affirmations

I behave as an equal to all persons.

I am smart.

I am intelligent.

I am knowledgeable.

I am competent.

I accept my goodness.

I am perfect, just as I am.

There is nothing I can do, say, think, or become that establishes my worth, my self-worth comes from God.

# Chapter 3

## The Past Revisited

The American culture has many generalized erroneous perceptions of the African American that are negative, limited, restrictive, fear-laden, and stereotypical.

The modern day African American is a product of the African culture on the continent of Africa and a complex mixture of the confederate south. Most of the slaves were separated from their families and sold individually rather than as a family. After they were established in the home of a slave master, many had kind slave masters, but most experienced abuse. All slaves were not respected; thought to be stupid and without intelligence. They came from different tribes and spoke the language of their tribe. They did not know how to speak, or read English. Most of them were forbidden to learn to read. Many caring children sneaked and taught slave children how to read. Some Africans, like Phyllis Wheatley, learned to read on their own. This gave them a feeling of competence, self-respect, and added to their positive self-image and self-esteem.

The African settlers to America were uprooted from their families on both shores of Africa, and after they arrived in the United States. They were thought to be child-like, unintelligent, easy to scare, wild, and like untamed animals. They were placed in chains and, like an animal, sold on an auction block. This was degrading and dehumanizing. It accomplished the intended objective which was to instill fear, inferiority, and the mind set of servitude and enslavement. In addition, whites were considered the elite, and slaves were thought of as monetary property. They were valued for their brute strength and ability to work long hours in the sun. Slaves did not have the right to disagree with a request or demand made upon them; neither could they refuse the demand of anyone who was white, even if the person was a child.

Angela Davis, in **Women, Race and Class**, wrote, "females, slave women were inherently vulnerable to all forms of sexual coercion. The most violent punishments of men consisted of flogging (beatings), and mutilations. Most women were flogged, mutilated, and raped. Rape was a camouflaged expression of the slave holders' economic mastery, and the overseers' control of Black women as workers."

In 1860, there were 488,070 free African Americans and 4 million enslaved Africans in America. Most of them could not read or write, and had to learn any way they could. They used the Bible or relied on abolitionists – people who were against slavery – and young white children. Many stole books from the private libraries of their masters, or whites who employed them. And they sought out other African Americans who could read and write.

According to Carter G. Woodson's **The Negro in Our History**, in the 1700s Harry and Andrew, last name unknown, started a school for slaves in Goose Creek Parish in South Carolina, and became the first African Americans employed as teachers.

During the early years of America's history, skin color was not as important as it has since become. As the country grew, rich white land owners decided to institute a more profitable employment system called slavery. Africans were forced to become slaves. The white men who established the system declared Africans as inferior and sub-human, and skin color became the most important human characteristic in America.

Color of skin determined who received respect, who was important, and who was treated as a person. A person's self-worth was based on skin color, and all Africans were treated as children and thought to be childlike. Slaves were forbidden to learn to read or write. Therefore the self-esteem and self-image of the African American is rooted in shame about their skin color, and self-doubt about their intelligence or ability to think.

African Americans have always been valued for what they did, not for who they were. So one's ability to make a worthwhile contribution to humanity has always been associated with who one was, and how one performed. African American women, men, and children were treated like children regardless of their age. And all whites were considered to be their masters.

African Americans of all ages, called white children "mister" and "miss". This practice added to the destruction of their sense of self-worth, self-appreciation, and self-respect.

It is self-degrading for an adult Black man to say "yes, sir" and "no ma'am" to a child, perhaps the same age as his own child, who he expects to respect him. To act in this manner put the man on the same level as his child, and reinforces the notion that he is half a man. A man-child is not a real man because he has no control over his life, his family's welfare, or the circumstances that confront them. My father was placed in this situation as a child. It made him very strict and demanding of respect from the five of us kids as well as my mother.

In the past, and still today, the Black man thirsts for self-respect and has a shattered, distorted self-concept and self-image. Any attempts to develop self-respect or self-pride were further eroded through institutionalized separatism of the races. This separation between Blacks and Whites, for instance, existed at public water fountains.

In Pensacola, Florida where I grew up, Blacks were not allowed to eat at the lunch counter with whites. We attended separate schools, lived in separate neighborhoods, and we had to sit in the back seats of all public transportation. The signs read "white" and "colored." This was a normal practice in Pensacola until a little over 25 years ago. This is why I find myself struggling at time with low self-esteem, feelings of low self-worth, and a distorted self-image that tells me I am inferior to whites.

People cannot be chained in shackles all their lives, then abruptly have the physical shackles removed and told they are free human beings, adults, no longer "children," and should begin to think, and behave as independent free adults.

It is easy to remove a physical shackle or chain; however, it may take centuries to unchain a shackled mind. The mind and psyche of all

African Americans, whether they lived in the liberal North, or in the Ku-Klux Clan confederate south, continue to be shackled and chained due to years of conditioning.

All African Americans living in the south lived in fear of over-stepping their boundaries, of getting out of their place, and being reminded through a stare, a cold shoulder treatment, or through emotional isolation, that they were still sub-human and undeserving of respect as a human being.

It is very challenging to remove the mental, or emotional shackles of an enslaved mind that send out continual messages: "Beat up on me," "I am not OK, but you are OK," "I am worthless," "I need someone other than myself to validate me," "I am not sure if I am as smart as whites, or other races of people," "I can't think to figure things out for myself, I need to use the brains of someone other than myself," "My brains are no good, and will therefore not work for me," "I am not as valuable as whites," "I am stupid," "I am inferior," "My mind won't work for me," "You do not like my looks, and neither do I," "My skin color is dark, my lips are thick, my nose is wide and large, I do not look like those I see on television or on the magazine covers – I am different," "I wish my skin color was lighter, " "There is something abnormal about my skin coloration." When we were children, innocently playing, we stated this phrase to each other on a daily basis, "If you are brown stick around, if you are black, step back, if you are white, you are alright." All of these are self-denial and self-rejection phrases.

I remember as a teenager, buying a container of skin bleaching cream to lighten my skin. Even though I was a pretty shade of brown, I did not see nor acknowledge this to myself, until I was told this by a white friend.

In Florida, where I grew as a teenager, I could not be seen playing with my white friend. It was acceptable with her mother for us to be friends; however she asked that we not be seen together in public because she feared what might happen to her daughter. I was thought to be inferior to a fourteen-year-old white girl. Can you imagine the emotional scarring an innocent action like this produces? I have been working on my self-esteem ever since I left Florida, healing one layer at a time.

Due to the conditioning factor of spaced repetition our mind remembers and retains what it hears. Our minds retain all information, whether it is to our benefit or not. You only need to reject yourself once, to set in motion self-denial, self-rejection patterns. Blacks are ridiculed, and humiliated by whites and other races of people. And we in turn ridicule, humiliate, and reject ourselves, and other Blacks. This is a behavior we need to be mindful to avoid.

Some Blacks who had a lighter complexion were accepted more readily by whites. This was especially true if they were able to work and buy their freedom.

Some African Americans bought their freedom from their slave master. An industrious and persevering individual was Alonzo Herndon, who lived from 1858 to 1927, and turned $11 in savings into a fortune to become America's first African American millionaire. He started as a barber with white only clients. He wrote, *"I started out alone with a five-chair shop and by unceasing watchfulness of my business and tactful, I hope, manly conduct toward my Southern patrons with whom I am happy to say, I have always had the most pleasant esteem and have every reason to believe my business is held...I have grown from five barber chairs to twenty-five employing nearly forty men."* When the state passed a law in 1905 requiring that insurance companies deposit $5,000 with the state treasurer, Mr. Herndon purchased nine small burial associations and organized them into the Atlanta Mutual Insurance Association which later became the Atlanta Life Insurance Company, now the second largest African American Life Insurance Company in the nation. Atlanta Life provided insurance and mortgages to low-income Blacks who were unable to obtain the services elsewhere. The company also provided professional, managerial and clerical jobs to African Americans. Mr. Herndon was worth $1.1 million at the time of his death in 1927.

Children as well as adults learn from society about their self-worth, self-image, and self-importance. If references have been made, and put in print, that they have the brain of an ape, that they are the offspring of a gorilla, that their brain mass is smaller than that of whites, if everything said about them in books is negative or degrading, they will eventually believe it. Also if a person is told or made to believe a given statement is factual, even though it may be a conjecture with limited evidential fact, it will be accepted as true by the mind. This is especially true if the information is stated over a medium such as television.

Our self-esteem is a blueprint of who we are, how we have been treated, respected, appreciated, and identified by those around us and our external family. The self-image is a by-product of the self-esteem. It reflects how we picture ourselves, shows how we respect and value ourselves. It paints a mental picture from our inner beliefs of who we think we can be or what we believe we can do in life.

Your self-esteem tells whether you like yourself. You can have a high self-esteem and be unsuccessful in school, or mathematics, because your concept of self-worth is not related to your education or academics. Your criteria of success, be it sports, music, education, or business determines your self-esteem factor. You will need to tie your sense of self-worth/importance to whatever it is you aspire to achieve or accomplish. If your high self-esteem is based on success in athletics or on relationships, you will be successful in sports and as a "social butterfly" and a failure in scholastics, or academically. Your self-esteem is multi-faceted, expansive and changes continually as you evolve.

Your self-image is the picture you hold in your mind about who you think you are. We see from the inside out. You act and behave based on the pictures you now hold in your mind. When you change the image on the picture frame in your mind, you change your self-image. Your self-image and your every day habits are intertwined. Change one and you will automatically change the other.

African American children need a more developed feeling of identity, to see themselves in the light of the historic contributions of their ancestors. This will help them develop a greater appreciation for the chronological role, and impact each category of individuals has had on their life.

In the list below, write what each person did, if you are unsure, go to a library or the internet and look up each name:

## 1. Slaves – Emancipators

Fredrick Douglass ...........................................................

Harriet Tubman  ...........................................................

Sojourner Truth  ...........................................................

Nat Turner  ...........................................................

Phyllis Wheatley  ...........................................................


## 2. Negro – Scholars

Booker T. Washington  ...........................................................

George Washington Carver  ...........................................................


## 3. Medicine – Physician

Eliza Anna Grier  ...........................................................

Dr. Daniel Hale Williams  ...........................................................


## 4. Educators

Mary Jane Patterson  ...........................................................

Mary McCleod Bethune Cookman  ...........................................................

Dr. Benjamin Mays  ...........................................................


## 5. Politics

Adam Clayton Powell  ...........................................................

Shirley Chisholm  ...........................................................

Dr. Ralph Bunche ...........................................................

Ron Brown  ...........................................................

Barack Obama  ...........................................................

## 6. **Sports**

## 7. **Business**

## 8. **Motion Pictures**

## 9. **Publishers**

## 10. **Entertainment – Jazz**

James Baldwin .................................................................

Dr. Frances Cress Welsing.............................................

## 15. **Ballet**
Alvin Ailey Dance Troupe............................................

## 16. **Opera**
Leontyne Price .............................................................

Marion Anderson .........................................................

## 17. **Gospel Music**
Mahalia Jackson...........................................................

Sister Rosetta Tharpe ..................................................

Five Blind Boys ...........................................................

Soul Stirrers ...............................................................

Pilgrim Travelers .........................................................

Aretha Franklin...........................................................

## 18. **Music Composition**
Thomas Dorsey ...........................................................

## 19. **Civil Rights Activist**
Dr. Martin Luther King Jr. ...........................................

Rosa Parks .................................................................

Reverend Jesse Jackson .................................................

Reverend Al Sharpton ..................................................

## 20. **Supreme Court Justice**
Thurgood Marshall ......................................................

## 21. **Chemist**
Drew Scott .................................................................

Percy Lavon Julian.......................................................

## 22. Journalist & Social Worker
Victoria Earle Matthews ...............................................

## 23. Social Reform
Dorothy Height, NCNW ...............................................

The above exercise is intended to instill pride in you for your rich diverse cultural heritage. With respect, appreciation and understanding for the people who paved the path, and paid an enormous price for the racial legacy you enjoy today. Write your comments below about how you feel.

Now take this quick quiz. Using a sheet of paper, list three categories and see if you remember three people in them. For example, Emancipator, Medicine, and Opera

There are many talented, educated African Americans who were trail blazers for the African American child today. One such person is Mary McLeod Bethune, who founded Bethune Cookman College in Daytona Beach, Florida. She wrote a living legacy of principles to guide African American youths. *"If I have a legacy to leave my people, it is my philosophy of living and serving. I pray that my philosophy may be helpful to those who share my vision of a world of peace."*

*"Here, then is my legacy...*
*I leave you love. I leave you hope. I leave you the challenge of developing confidence in one another. I leave you a thirst for education. I leave you a respect for the use of power. I leave you faith. I leave you racial dignity. I leave you a desire to live harmoniously with your fellow men. I leave you finally a responsibility to our young people."*
— MARY MCLEOD BETHUNE COOKMAN

*One cannot understand the present unless one understand the past.*
– Yehudah Leib Eiger of Lublin,
Nineteenth Century Hasidic Rabbi

*A people trained for generations in the house of bondage cannot cast off in an instant the effects of that training and become truly free, even when the chains have been struck off.*
– Ahad Ha-am, Asher Hirsch Ginsberg,
Early Twentieth Century Hebrew Essayist

*As long as a person breathes that person should not lose hope.*
– Jerusalem Talmud 9, 1

*A negligent man starves in the midst of abundance.*
– Traditional Sayings of African Peoples Baya

*If you don't plant in summer, what will you get in winter?*
Midrash to Proverbs

**To know your true self, answer these questions**

1. Who am I?
   I am:  ................................................................

2. What I really want to be/have in life is:

   ................................................................

   ................................................................

3. Finish this statement,
   "I am most unhappy *at home* when I have to / need to…"

66

4. Finish this statement, "I am the happiest *at home* when I..."

## SELF-ESTEEM, THE ESSENCES OF YOU
### Assimilation-→ Integration/Embarrassment-→ Shame-→ Confusion-→ Feelings of Less Than

A. Which category/ies has had a negative effect on developing your self-esteem?

B. State how this has influenced your personal life/school.

### African Proverbs
*The ruin of a nation begins in the homes of its people.*
ASHANTI

### Light The Fire Within You™

**To discover your passion in life, ask yourself these question**
1. What things in life give you the greatest pleasure or satisfaction? Write these down then put them in order 1, 2 etc.

Personal:

Future Career Goals:


Social:


Spiritual:


2. What things do others praise or compliment you on? List below:


3. Now that you have completed the activities above, what thing or things would you enjoy doing every day of the year, even if you were not paid monetarily?



Whatever you choose as your passion, (your hot button); start now and enjoy the rest of your life.

### *Life Is Shorter Than You Think.*

### I Am Worth It

I *may sometime cause confusion when I am unclear in my communication, unsure of myself, or uncertain about an outcome, yet I am worth the bother.*
I *may act timid and fearful sometimes, but please remember that I am trying to sort things out in my mind, and I am worth the bother.*
*Even though you may struggle to understand me, I am worth it.*
*My friend, I am the other half of you.*

68

*I am incomplete without you, and you are incomplete without me.*
*In some strange way, though we differ in racial composition,*
*thoughts, ideas, and behavior; we are wedded to each other.*
*I will release you for now, to soar above the heavens. Just remem-*
*ber that whatever disappointment or challenge I face, I deserve*
*the best, for I am worth it.*

– IDA GREENE

**SELF-ESTEEM – ARE YOU READY TO CHANGE?**

1.  State how you can change the following:
    a.  Your beliefs (thoughts) –


    b.  Your Self-Respect –


    c.  Your Attitude from negative to positive –


    d.  Self-Image to match person you desire to become –


    e.  Self-Acceptance/Appreciation, state what you will do –


    f.  How will you change self-defeating behaviors like procrastination, tardiness, or boredom? –


    g.  To have more energy and feel alive, avoid the 3 Cs:
        • **C**riticizing –
        • **C**omplaining –
        • **C**ondemning –

2. To experience more happiness, eliminate the following. Write what you will do to control or eliminate:
   a. Resentment – I will control resentment by


   b. Envy – I will control envy by:


   c. Jealousy – I will control jealousy by:


   d. Frustration→Irritation→ Anger→ Hostility→
      • Rage: I will stop the cycle at the above point:


Anger can be used by others to confuse or control you. In conflict, resolution anger is a useful emotion when used to support yourself against attack by others to over power or control you. Anger takes away energy, because it emotionally charges you, even when it is used constructively because of its potential to destroy others' self-confidence, anger must be under your control. Anger can be like an atomic bomb when uncontrolled.

---

**Anger Can Be Used By Others To Confuse and Control You**

Conflict resolution **Anger** is useful
when used to support yourself against abuse.
ANGER is always a loss of energy

---

Anger is triggered by external events called provocations. These create anger thoughts, anger arousal, and anger actions, which all escalate each other until they are fused together, like the three prongs on a pitchfork, in an anger feedback loop that leads to destructive consequences. The thickness of the lines indicates the increasing fusion; the thicker they are, the more intense the anger feedback loops, and the harder it is to break. As the center of the triangle gets smaller, the fusion is greater, making productive actions harder to generate. Productive actions cannot be made when the anger feedback loop is completely fused. Working it out prevents total fusions.

## How (conflict) emotional anger works

A. Provocation-→ Angry Thoughts You Create-→Expectations-→ Unfulfilled Need

B. Action (your response to unmet need) → Arousal-→ (what you do to fix the problem)

C. Therefore to change your angry feelings, you must change your thoughts before your behavior will change.

### Steps to learn self-control

1. Notice when you are too hyperactive and unable to focus your thoughts (attention) or energy (nervous, fidgety).

2. When you are too hyperactive to think, or be calm, take deep breaths, breathe deeply for three minutes or count to ten, three times.

3. Learn to organize you immediate environment by keeping things in order. Put things back as you find them, to help create order and stability for yourself.

4. Work to be a thinker, rather than an emotional reactor.

5. When you need to make a decision, give yourself two choices before you decide.

6. Pay attention to your feelings. Remember to validate them by asking yourself the following key questions:
   a. What am I feeling?

   b. Why am I feeling this way?

   c. What are the precipitating circumstances causing me to feel this way?

   d. How often do I feel this way?

   e. Who am I emulating, mom, dad, grandmother, grandfather, aunt, uncle?

7. Listen more intently to what the other person is saying to you, and ask for clarification if you are unsure. Also do the following:

   a. Listen with the intent to understand.
   b. Always repeat back to the other person in your own words what you think you heard them say.
   c. As a double check for listening, state "I am asking for clarification to be sure I heard you correctly, did you I hear you say ..............................................................?

## SELF-ESTEEM, How to Control an Angry Person

1.  When the person is exploding, maintain eye contact and just listen.
2.  Distance yourself at least four arm lengths away from the person.
3.  Remain calm-stand or sit still.
4.  Assume an "open" posture with your hands.
5.  Speak softly when the other person's voice is raised.
6.  Call the person by name
7.  When in disagreement: Do not touch, point, order, scold, challenge, interrupt, argue, belittle, intimidate, or threaten the angry person.
8.  Acknowledge the other person's feelings, express regret about the problem if appropriate.
9.  Get permission to ask questions.
10. Find out what was the triggering event, and if there are underlying feelings such as fear, anxiety, humiliation, or frustration.
11. Help the person get control over the situation by asking questions, or offering solutions.

*God gives blessings to all men.*
*If man had to distribute them, many would go without*
Traditional Sayings of African Peoples
HAUSA

## Self Quiz to Manage Your Anger

1.  What is your definition of anger?
    a.  Is it a good feeling, or bad feeling?

2.  Describe your bodily reactions when you get angry. E.g. The tightness of your throat when you are scared

3. Are you able to think about your bodily reactions when you are angry? Explain –

4. Are you able to think about what caused you to get/be angry before you react?

5. Are you ready to stop being an angry person? Do you want to change the way you react?

6. What do you feel when you are angry? Explain in details.
   a. Out of control

   b. Powerful

   c. Powerless

7. Are you in touch with the dark side of yourself? Did you know you were capable of having these feelings/emotions? When did you last have the feelings below?
   a) Resentment -
   b) Envy -
   c) Jealousy -
   d) Feelings of Loss -
   e) Fear -

## THINK BEFORE YOU ACT
### Let's Take Action Now

Use this problem solving technique to help you with a current problem.
State your problem

..............................................................................

..............................................................................

..............................................................................

Outline your response. ....................................................

..............................................................................

..............................................................................

..............................................................................

List your alternatives

..............................................................................

..............................................................................

..............................................................................

## Write out and visualize the consequences
Strategy 1:

..............................................................................

..............................................................................

| Positive Consequences | Negative Consequences |
|---|---|
| ............................................. | ............................................. |
| ............................................. | ............................................. |
| ............................................. | ............................................. |
| ............................................. | ............................................. |
| ............................................. | ............................................. |

Strategy 2:

.....................................................................................

.....................................................................................

| Positive Consequences | Negative Consequences |
|---|---|
| ............................................. | ............................................. |
| ............................................. | ............................................. |
| ............................................. | ............................................. |
| ............................................. | ............................................. |
| ............................................. | ............................................. |

## Affirmation for Self-Control

*My peace is within me, and is not disturbed by anything outside of me. I am in control of my thoughts, my feelings and my reactions. I develop a habit of being mindful, whereby I remember to be aware of myself when I am provoked, and consciously refrain from over-reacting.*

*I have a right to my opinion, but I do not have the right to inflict anger upon another person. And I no longer wish to inflict it on myself. I intend to heal myself of this problem, and I accept my healing now.*

## Thought for the Day

*Flatter me, and I may not believe you.*
*Criticize me, and I may not like you.*
*Ignore me, and I may not forgive.*
*Encourage me, and I will not forget you.*
— ANON

## Prayer of Faith

*God is my help in every need,*
*God does my every hunger feed.*
*God walks besides me, guides my way*
*Through every moment of the day.*
*I now am wise, I now am true.*
*Patient, kind, and loving too.*
*All things I am can do and be,*
*Through Christ, the truth that is in me.*
*God is my health, I can't be sick.*
*God is my strength, unfailing, quick.*
*God is my all, I know no fear,*
*Since God and love and truth are here.*
— HANNAH MORE KOHAUS

## Managing Your Anger

*They learn that those who lose their temper lose and that if you have a sense of humor you will be unstoppable.*
— ANON

*A weak person goes where he is smiled at.*
Traditional Sayings of African Peoples
HERRO

**Affirmations**

*My way in life is made clear to me,*
*I listen to, and follow my intuition.*
*I am filled with enthusiasm, and*
*I am an enthusiastic person.*

– IDA GREENE

*Light The Fire Within You*™
*Self-Esteem, The Essence Of You*

1. Things I like about myself:



   Because…



2. Things I dislike about myself:



   Because…



3. To discover your strengths:
   State/list characteristics or traits that are uniquely you.

4. To find your weaknesses:
   List faults or areas of your personality you want to improve.



5. To enhance your self-image:
   Ask yourself "How do I see myself in relation to others, am I as good?" State in what way you are better, in relation to a:
   a) Dog –


   b) Ant –


   c) Butterfly –


   d) Worm –


## CHANGE YOUR THINKING TO
### *Light the Fire within You*™

**Things I will change as of today**
*I now affirm that:*
   I like me!
   I like the person I am becoming.
   I trust my judgment.
   I trust my decision making ability.
   I know my mind is as good as that of others. I accept that my mind will work for me.
   I know I can make wise decisions.
   I have an excellent memory.

79

I can depend on my mind to remember things.

I can figure things out with my keen, sharp, mind.

I now release anger, resentment, and all past unhappy thoughts.

It is O.K. for me to make a mistake.

It is O.K. for me to not be perfect.

It is O.K. for me to relax.

It is O.K. for me to be me.

It is O.K. for me to not know everything.

It is O.K. for me to be corrected or get advice about myself.

It is O.K. for me to be Happy.

**SECONDARY FACTORS THAT AFFECT OUR SELF-ESTEEM**

1. Listening Skills – Hear new information, decide to act/not act,
2. Shame – Feel shy or self-conscious,
3. Rejection – Lack of approval/self-dislike, low/no self-concept,
4. Ridicule – To feel blame or embarrassment with reason,
5. Fear/Intimidation – Anxiety about a real/imagined harm,
6. Confusion – Behaviors I do the lead to disapproval/rejection,
7. Low/No Self-Respect – Use of words that show low self-regard, inability to esteem oneself,
8. A "Something for Nothing" belief, allows one to be tricked, or be misled
9. Criticism-disapproves/finds fault, judge self-and others
10. Lack of self-discipline – No control over one's mouth, self-interest and rebellious actions,
11. Intolerance/Impatience – Hot tempered, easy to anger/offend,
12. Lack of Affection/Caring – Inability to feel or express feelings,
13. Lack of Security-Inability to trust self-or others,
14. Lack of Encouragement or Praise-creates low self-worth,
15. Low Self-appreciation – Unsure of self, feelings of injustice, unfairness,
16. Assimilate – Integration into a group/culture that does not accept you.

Write which of the above has affected your self-esteem, and what you will do to change this.

**Look in the Mirror Every Morning and Affirm:**

1. I nurse my inner child with love in my heart, and I am healed of past errors.
2. I now support my inner child. I am healed of any sense of low self-worth. I am worthy and deserving of all the good I can imagine and then more.
3. It is o.k. for the little child in me to succeed and be successful.
4. I approve of my inner child, she/he is o.k.
5. I am a spiritual being living a spiritual life. There is no place for doubt, anxiety, or fear.
6. Knowing that what I experience is a result of my thinking; I eliminate all negativity from my mind. I accept the good that I desire.
7. I perceive the truth that I live in a spiritual universe, and by seeing myself as a spiritual being I have dominion over all of my life.
8. I have that within me which will maintain and sustain me in all ways, for I and my Father/Mother God are one.
9. I am blessed with an abundance of all the good life has to offer, this includes money, and money substance.
10. I rejoice that I am both a child of God and a child of earth, that all of life, both divine and human, is mine to live and enjoy.
11. I rely on the spirit of self-reliance within me to satisfy all my needs.

# Chapter 4

## How to Improve Self-Esteem
## in the African American Child

Children are open and loving. They lack the skills to nurture, to protect, or to maintain their sense of self-against subtle or open bias, exclusivity, or rejection. Children must first like, respect and appreciate themselves before they can do this for another human being.

Self-esteem is not a privilege, it is a right. However, African American children struggle on a daily basis to keep and maintain their cultural identity or sense of self.

To improve self-esteem in the African American, we need to understand the factors responsible for the problem. Oppressed group behavior has been observed in colonized Africans, Jews in Nazi Germany, Hispanic-Americans, and African Americans. This syndrome appears when one group is controlled by another group when it is perceived as having more power and influence. Oppression leads to certain behavior patterns, including low self-esteem, horizontal violence, and passive-aggressive behavior.

Horizontal violence is aggression directed at one's peers because it cannot be taken out on those with power. Among Blacks this may manifest as: lack of trust, suspicion, negative comments, prejudicial remarks, or degrading statements made about Blacks when in the presence of whites, or other races. Low self-esteem can manifest in someone who is apathetic and doesn't try, due to feelings of hopeless, and helplessness.

Other factors that cause low self-esteem in African Americans are:
1. Feelings that they are not good enough for God to care about.
2. Ignorance about their culture
3. Lack of awareness about the history of Blacks. And the institutional racial discrimination, prejudice, and lives lost for them to enjoy the freedom they have today.
4. The lack of respect for life, particular their own. Easy access of

weapons to destroy life; violence against each other occurs you are disrespected or embarrassed. However, at the Million Man March, many gang leaders vowed to end their anger and violent acts towards each other.

5.  Music on radio and MTV-lyrics are explicit and say unflattering things about African American females. Sexual activity is explicitly suggestive to young children.

6.  Use of abusive language when addressing each other is derogatory and belittling (calling other Blacks "Nigger," "Blood"). African Americans were called "Niggers," by racist whites who refused to call them Negro.

7.  Increased use of alcohol and experimental drug use among young people.

8.  Lack of strong extended family ties. Family members living in different cities, prevent the close monitoring of inappropriate or deviant behavior.

9.  Lack of respect for elders and their knowledge.

10. Increase in television watching has a higher priority than homework study time.

11. Low interest in going to college among high school students.

12. Inability of both boys and girls to curb sexual activity before marriage. The message used to be "no sex until adulthood and then sex in a committed relationship." Both young males and females seem to have no control over their sexual urges. Whatever the reason, there is a lack of sexual restraint. The motto seems to be "if it feels good do it," and "do your own thing."

13. Lack of knowledge about love. The practice of young girls to get pregnant to have someone, "love them." It is the nature of babies to receive love, not give love. If a baby receives love as a child, it is less likely to look outside itself for the love it already has.

14. Increase in suicide rate among teenagers. Although the rate is not as high for African Americans as others races, the loss of any African American teenager is a tragedy. It has passed down through

the generations of religious upbringing for Blacks, that suicide is the one unpardonable sin.

15. Lastly, the strong religious upbringing for African Americans. Jesus has been the central focus in the life of African Americans for years. Religion has kept the Black community together. Today many young people are not encouraged to go to church. Sports, is rapidly taking a higher place in the life and affairs of African American youth, than religion.

Traditions are the tools the youth of today need to maintain the transfer of knowledge from generation to generation. Children cannot talk to a football, basketball, or baseball athlete about their problems. Nor can they speak to a television about their tradition and culture. All traditional information about one's culture is shared verbally, through example or experience. This knowledge is stored in the mind, and heart of our elders.

Wisdom is learned knowledge. It can be taught and passed on to those willing to grasp its fruit. You will find in life that there are two kinds of lessons; those that can be **taught** and those that need to be **bought**. The lessons you **buy** are the most heart wrenching, because you learn them the hard way. You pay an emotional, physical, or spiritual price for every lesson you learn this way. You may tell an untruth to your mom or dad and get away with it. However, if you tell an untruth at school, it may cause harm to another or harm to yourself. If you are suspended from school for a week, it may cause you to feel embarrassed, humiliated, and lower your self-worth/self-esteem.

If you steal, you could be caught by the police and taken to juvenile hall/court. Some children can be told that it is wrong to lie or steal and they avoid doing the misdeed; yet others will have to learn from trial and error. Cultural traditions act as a guide for right behavior, Thessalonians 2:15, says, "*Stand fast and hold the traditions which ye have been taught.*" There is an increasing trend among African American youths to ignore the courtesies, manners and respect, practiced by the older generation, calling these practices old fashioned. In the past "drugs" were never seen as a "God," to solve personal problems as practiced today. Jesus and prayer was the solution to every problem.

Traditions are a useful way to impart knowledge from the past. On the continent of Africa, cultural traditions have a "Rites of Passage" ceremony which a young boy and girl complete as they make the transition from childhood to woman/manhood. I have developed a modified program called "The Many Faces of You," whereby young children ages 6–18 complete a 14-week series of structured classes, designed to help them identify areas of their life that need improvement or corrective action. The program is threefold: covering the 14 characteristics of high self-esteem, the Ten Commandments, and 12 African values one needs to master before reaching adulthood.

## THE 14 CHARACTERISTICS OF A PERSON WITH HIGH SELF-ESTEEM

1. **Respect** – for self-and others, reverence for all life or life forms like (animals, birds, and insects). The ability to hold in high regard the wisdom of elders and their knowledge, achievements and accomplishments, to let it serve as a guideline for oneself. Wisdom is the ability to profit from the life experiences and mistakes of others.

2. **Loving** – Congenial, cooperative, compliant, teachable. Be in control of your mood and temper; to be cordial, agreeable, and polite.

3. **Dependable** – Reliable, to show up on time.

4. **Honest** – To not steal or take what is not yours.

5. **Commitment** – keep your word or follow through on what you say. The ability to commit, honor your obligations.

6. **Truth** – Tell the truth regardless of consequences to self

7. **Self-Appreciation** – Self-acceptance, know and accept one's strengths/weakness, use of boundaries to support one values, self-acknowledgement, be one's own best friend, to like oneself; to be able to receive and give a compliment.

8. **Integrity** – Have a sense of right and wrong, respect the rights and property of others, do what is right for self-and others.

9.  **Self-Worth** – Positive self-regard with a set of values to live by, accept themselves and others as a child of God; does not seek to be like others, or compare self-with others; feel valuable or worthwhile, ability to turn one's weaknesses into strengths.

10. **Responsible** – Self-reliance, industrious; your positive behavior matches your words. Look for ways to improve yourself and your life; being willing to take the necessary steps to provide for your livelihood.

11. **Trustworthy** – Can be trusted to follow through on what they start, able to follow directions.

12. **Consistent** – You are the same all the time, at home or away from home.

13. **Self-Confidence** – Courage, ability to take risks and be uncomfortable, ability to cope with disappointment, adversity, failure, and discouragement, without giving up on yourself.

14. **Positive Attitude** – To have a "Yes, I can attitude," to believe in the goodness of all people without cynicism or arrogance.

### REMEMBER

I told you earlier that to have self-confidence you need a **TAB** (see page 10)

**T**hink Confident – "Can Do" Attitude

**A**ct Confident

**B**e Confident

### WHAT YOU CAN DO TO CHANGE YOUR SELF-CONFIDENCE
**You have control over, and can change, the following:**

1.  **Your Attitude** – It tells how you feel about yourself.
    a.  Positive attitude builds self-confidence
    b.  Negative attitude tear down self-confidence

2.  **Your Environment** – The friends you choose reflect your self-image.

3.  **Your Learning Skills** – Knowing how you receive and

communicate information to help you learn faster.

a. ***Visual Person*** – Learns through seeing
b. ***Auditory Person*** – Learns through hearing
c. ***Kinesthetic Person*** – Learns through moving, doing, and touching

Finish This Sentence – I Am Special Because…

A.

B.

C.

## *Each One Reach One*
## *Each One Teach One*
### IDA GREENE

Our culture gives us information about our ancestors, family members who lived before us. Our culture helps us create a point of reference as the beginning of you. It provides an identity for us of how those who look like us began. It gives us a map to follow, and shows us how to begin. When the child is young, it seeks a point of reference as the beginning of self: Where did I come from? To whom do I belong? How did I get to earth? Are there other people who look like me? Our cultural ethnic identity answers this question. Write any thoughts that come to your mind here:

Write any thoughts or feelings you have about your family members. Who do you feel has contributed positively to your self-esteem and self-confidence, why?

A. Write about the accepted values in the home of your family or culture: What you could or could not do or say.

.......................................................................

.......................................................................

.......................................................................

.......................................................................

B. Is there something missing in your life, if so what is it? Can you do anything to fill this void, so it does not take from your self-esteem?

.......................................................................

.......................................................................

.......................................................................

.......................................................................

**Always Live Life to the Fullest**
**A GUIDE TO SELF-ESTEEM**

*Don't let go of hope.*
*Hope gives you the strength to keep going*
*When you feel like giving up.*
*Don't ever quit believing in yourself.*
*As long as you believe you can,*
*You will have a reason for trying.*
*Don't let anyone hold your happiness in their hands;*
*Hold it in yours, so it will always be within your reach.*
*Don't measure success or failure by material wealth,*

*But by how you feel;*
*Our feelings determine the richness of our lives.*
*Don't let bad moments overcome you;*
*We all need it from time to time.*
*Don't run away from love but towards love,*
*because it is our deepest joy.*
*Don't wait for what you want to come to you.*
*Go after it with all that you have, knowing that life will meet you halfway.*
*Don't feel like you've lost, when plans and dreams fall short of your hopes.*
*Anytime you learn something new about yourself or about life, you have*
*  progressed.*
*Don't do anything that takes away from your self-respect.*
*Feeling good about your self-is essential to feeling good about life.*
*Don't ever forget how to laugh or be too proud to cry.*
*It is by doing both that we live life to its fullest.*

– NANCYE SIMS

## TWENTY LAWS OF SELF-ESTEEM

1.  Accept yourself confidently as you are.
2.  Never do anything in private that you would not want the world to know.
3.  Think the best, and expect the best, of yourself at all times.
4.  Become your own best friend.
5.  Perform to the best of your ability in all your endeavors.
6.  Put no other person before you; including your friend, child, mother, father, lover, husband, or wife.
7.  Develop and nourish your inner-self continuously.
8.  Listen and be open to your inner prompting and follow your intuition.
9.  Hold yourself in high esteem and accept that there is a larger force in the universe that operates independent of you.
10. Know that there is a force that keeps the universe together, and that all things are always working out as they should.

11. Think for yourself, trust your judgment, and make your own decisions.
12. Worry less and trust your decision making ability.
13. Become a decision maker.
14. Be a mover and doer of goodwill for yourself and all humanity.
15. Treat yourself with kindness, dignity and self-respect.
16. Guard the words that fall from your lips. Make them words of joy, happiness, goodwill towards all, including your self.
17. Avoid comparing yourself to others.
18. Expect the best from all people, including your self.
19. Constantly seek ways to improve yourself.
20. Strive for excellence in all you do, say, and think.

– IDA GREENE

## TEACHING THE AFRICAN AMERICAN CHILD TO LEARN

There are three levels of learning: literal, cognitive and evaluative.

**Literal** learning is specific, detailed, and simple. It is easy to understand because step A is connected to step B. There is a direct relationship between the two, it does not allow for variation, interpretation, ambiguity or change. Due to the practice of slavery African Americans needed to be sure they understood what was said to them, and not interpret or read anything into what was said to them, lest it be misinterpreted. Any actions or behavior they did could cause a reaction; result in overt hostility or punishment by the slave master. They also could be maimed, or killed, so they learned to express themselves in a specific, exact, and literal manner.

**Cognitive** learning deals with facts devoid of feeling states. The African American child's cultural orientation to the world is social and interactive. Therefore, they are unaccustomed to the cognitive individual style of learning. They also find it to be less socially engaging, not people oriented, hence no fun.

**Evaluative** learning involves the use of critical thinking skills. This way of learning could generate anxiety in someone who needs to be aware of every inflection of the words they say, lest it be misinterpreted, and cause them emotional pain or embarrassment.

Children fear rejection, they like safety. They want to be accepted and approved by their teachers. It is always safe to act in a culturally accepted manner, because our culture does not reject us, it supports us. Therefore, African American children learn in a style that is comfortable and non-threatening to them.

## WHAT THE AFRICAN AMERICAN CHILD CAN DO TO ENHANCE THEIR SELF-ESTEEM

Remember who you are; you are the child of a King, "God." You are royalty. God wants you to be the best and have the best. You have a rich cultural lineage of African ancestors who were Kings and Queens; therefore, you are a descendant of a living royal family. You came from a people who were proud of their heritage, the wisdom passed on to them, the color of their skin, a people who valued freedom, and were willing to die for it. You came from a people who viewed themselves as: just, compassionate, caring, and kind people; people, with a "big heart," who endured abuse, humiliation, and injustice, and still were willing to forgive those who hurt or abused them. You came from a people who were always ready to reach out to the less fortunate; those seen as the underdog, because they have been the under dog for centuries.

In addition to the things listed above, others things the African American child can do to enhance their self-esteem is to be in control of all toxic emotions. A toxic emotion is any emotion that has the potential to cause harm to another person, create disharmony between you and another, be a source of conflict, cause irreparable damage to a relationship, or destroy an interaction between you and another.

The following are emotions I consider toxic: Envy, Jealousy, Revenge, Fear, Hatred, and Anger. All of these emotions are addressed extensively in my book, Light the Fire Within You. Anger will be discussed here because it is often a cause for problems between African Americans and others. Blacks are perceived by the media as having dark,

91

sinister, vicious and violent natures. This mental programming creates fear in the mind of whites and non-whites when they encounter Blacks. It creates a stereotype that works to the disadvantage of Blacks. Because they are feared before they interact with others.

Anger is a chosen position. We can decide how we will react to a perceived threat to our ego, or emotional comfort. Anger is a signal for you, to look at what is going on in your emotions, and to find the cause of the anger.

Anger is a valuable signal, because it lets us know when something is wrong, and needs to be corrected. The critical factor is whether your expression of anger is adding to the problem rather than solving it.

**OFTEN WHEN WE ARE ANGRY, ONE OR MORE OF THESE THINGS ARE GOING ON:**
1. We want something and are not getting it.
2. From past experience, we expect trouble.
3. We have feelings of powerlessness.
4. We feel sadness
5. Feelings of grief, that take away our joy and feelings of aliveness.
6. Depression.
7. Feelings of negativity about life, self-and people.

In confronting anger, remember you have a choice; you have three options. 1. You can choose to react angrily, 2. Not react. 3. You can become aware of what you are feeling, aware of the intensity of your anger, aware if you are in control of your anger, or if your anger is in control of you.

Always assume responsibility for what you are feeling, and own all your feelings, including anger. Unresolved anger turns into resentment, envy, jealousy, revenge, and hatred. There is always an underlying feeling of inadequacy when you are angry. Anger moves through the following stages if it is not resolved immediately:

**Frustration→ Over Unmet Needs Disappointment→ Embarrassment→ Guilt→ Fear of Rejection**

1. **Frustration** – unfulfilled expectations. To prevent anger change your goal or plan
2. **Unmet Needs/Disappointment** – your unfulfilled expectations. To prevent anger, look into situation, get the facts.
3. **Embarrassment** – expected self-image unfulfilled. Solution: create new self-image
4. **Guilt** – social expectations you have accepted. Solution, confront the situation behavior or change it.
5. **Fear of rejection** – unknown expectations with probability of consequence. Solution: confront the situation/person/ behavior, explore the cause then decide if you want to avoid the behavior that causes the problem.

Anger is a waste of energy. It takes away your joy. It can be used by others to confuse or control you, if you are unaware of what you are feeling, unclear about what angers you, or have no control over your anger outburst. In conflict resolution anger is a useful emotion when used to support yourself against an attack by others to over power or control you.

**Learning to control your anger helps you**
1. **Recognize your temperament.**
2. **Validate your temperament.**
3. **Learn to delay action on your temper.**
4. **Label and verbalize your feelings.**
5. **Think about your options.**
6. **Empathize with others.**

When you develop inner control of a powerful emotion like anger, you become powerful. When you are controlled by your outer environment, you lose the opportunity to have inner control. To become good at any skill, whether it is controlling your expression of anger, or your tongue, requires continuous practice.

TEN STEPS TO CONTROL YOUR ANGER

1. **Make a list** of the things that make you mad, and memorize it.

2. **Talk about your feelings**, let people knows when things bother you.

3. **When you feel angry**, do something with the energy. Slowly breathe in and out ten times. On the exhale, spread your fingers apart widely and imagine the negative energy leaving your body as you do so.

4. **When you feel the urge to strike out at someone**, shrug (raise) your shoulders, as you breathe in deeply; rapidly lower your shoulders as you exhale. Notice your jaw muscles, shoulders, hands, chest, and torso muscles. Get in touch with what you are angry about, and with whom you are angry.

5. **Make peace with yourself** and the person who is the object of your anger. Forgive yourself first. Then apologize to the other person for your lack of control.

6. **Mentally visualize two paths**, (there is an exercise in my book *Light the Fire Within You*™, that teaches you how to visualize). Have one of these paths be positive, pleasant, and full of light. Have the other path be dark, gloomy, and depressive. Then send your angry feelings down the dark path and over the cliff.

7. **Notice if you feel like yelling**, screaming, or hitting. Before you act on your anger, think of why you are angry. Is your angry feeling legitimate, or did you create a situation to justify your need to be angry?

8. **Talk your way through your anger**. Tell yourself you can change from being a reactor of your emotions to being a processor. Notice your thoughts, change negative thoughts to positive.

9. **Change the image you have of yourself** from "blowing your stack, to being a cool headed person." Whenever you are able to control your anger, reinforce it by saying something kind to yourself.

10. **Daily seek ways to change** your image, inner thoughts, and outer behavior, so the two match.

ADDITIONAL THINGS YOU CAN DO TO CONTROL ANGER

11. **See yourself as a kind person**.

12. **Seek to become a thinker** rather than an emotional reactor. To be an emotional reactor is to be out of control of the self. An emotional reactor discharges and wastes valuable energy needed by the brain to process information When you are an emotional reactor you deplete your body of vital minerals and nutrients (calcium, protein, B complex vitamins, Vitamin C, zinc, manganese, potassium).

13. **Pay attention to your feelings**. Remember to validate your feelings by asking yourself these questions: "What am I feeling," "Why am I feeling this way?" " What were the precipitating circumstances to cause me to feel this way," "How often do I feel this way," and "Who am I emulating?"

14. **Work through negative emotions** as soon as they emerge.

15. Listen to hear what the other person is saying to you. When in doubt, ask for clarification.

16. **Listen with the intent to understand**. Repeat back to the other person in your words what you think you heard.

17. **Notice your body**, its space, the body of others and their space.

18. **Give others freedom of space** and they will honor your space.

In addition to learning to manage your anger, it is far better to *practice self-control*.

THE FOLLOWING SUGGESTIONS MAY HELP YOU

1. Work on being congruent on both inside and outside yourself.

2. Learn to organize your immediate environment.

3. Put things back as you find them to help create order and stability for yourself.

4. Seek to be the same all the time.

5. Learn to organize your life by keeping a daily "To Do List." Put all your daily activities into A, B, C, D, give "A" activities the highest priority, Bs next, etc.

6. Never settle for less than your best effort, best preparation and best outcome, preceded by your best follow through.
7. Be your own coach.
8. Push yourself to be your best, and tell yourself you can.
9. Others may provoke you to anger, but you do not have to respond angrily.
10. When you do what others want they have the power to control you.
11. No one is the cause of you responding angrily. You have freedom of choice.
12. When you get mad, you are exercising your power or seek to avenge yourself.
13. If you get angry repeatedly, you get some pleasure from hurting others.
14. If you get angry repeatedly, you are unable to control your feelings of anger.
15. To keep your anger under control, do a kind act each day for yourself and someone else.
16. Give yourself permission to be gentle with yourself and others, easy does it.
17. Practice ways to be gentle, and kind to yourself and others.
18. Do deep breathing exercises ten minutes, two times a day.
19. Learn to meditate, and practice it for twenty minutes, twice a day. The techniques on how to meditate are listed in my book *Light The Fire Within You*™.

You can use your ethnic pride as a tool to help you set goals, and feel proud of yourself.

Go through the exercises below to be in better control of your bothersome emotions. Have you ever felt any of the emotions below? Write about how they make you feel about yourself?

• Anger -

• Revenge -

• Jealousy -

• Resentment -

a. How do you feel after you have expressed the emotions above?

b. Do you feel happy, tired, or sad? Write about your feelings

c. Do you like the way you feel? (a desire to hurt others may indicate a need for professional counseling to help you cope with these feelings) Identify the words you use when interacting with others. For one week, monitor your inner self-talk and outer behavior. Write down your bodily reactions: breathing, clenched teeth, heavy breathing, tight neck or shoulder muscles, tight jaws, hot ears or other body parts, rigid, tense body posture, balled fist, rolled eyes. Write other bodily reactions you have that I did not list. Record your daily results below.

1. Day one:

2. Day two:

3.  Day three:

4.  Day four:

5.  Day five:

6.  Day six:

7.  Day seven:

**MOTHERS REAR SONS TO BE MEN**

This is a time of new beginnings for the black family. Many can now purchase items dreamed about. Overt discrimination against blacks is lessening. Many whites are seeking the friendship of blacks. With the influx of new minorities into the workforce many whites are attempting to align with African Americans as buffers to create a "we Americans" coalition against Asian newcomers to America. African Americans now have the purchasing power to travel abroad, and freedom to make large home improvements. It seems that we have come a long way; but have we, really? Teenage pregnancy is on the rise. Drug experimentation is starting at an earlier age; it affects all: lower, middle, and upper class, young, old, employed and unemployed. How can this tragedy occur in a family structure that was a haven of strong moral principles and values for African Americans, and Whites who had nannies or house-keepers?

Where did we go wrong? What has happened to the African American family? The problem can be traced to several factors: absence of the black male in the home (prison, incomplete parent training for the role of fatherhood), return of the mother to the work force, ruptured extended families (grandparents live in other parts of the city and country), young and immature family configuration, indifference, hopelessness, helplessness, lack of commitment, lack of self-discipline with sex organs leading to unplanned pregnancies and unwanted children, fear of responsibility, confusion between love and eroticism, separation between God and mankind, inability to incorporate spiritual principles into all facets of your life, living to impress people rather than God. All of these factors contribute to the breakdown of the African American family and this has a direct bearing on the transition from boy to manhood and child to adult.

For male children to avoid bad things, such as imprisonment, they must understand what behaviors, actions, and activities will land them in prison and what they can or should do if they are unjustly imprisoned. We must become proactive rather than reactive. We must learn to read, to understand the law and our protection under the law of the land.

African Americans need to form a coalition with the American Civil Liberties Union, and know when to seek the services of a competent lawyer, or the legal aid society if you have limited financial resources. Study and know the law. Know when your rights have been violated, what you must do, and how you must react to protect your rights as a citizen of the United States of America.

Self-esteem is not a privilege. It is a right. However, African American children struggle on a daily basis to keep and maintain their cultural identity, or sense of self. Children are open and loving. They lack the skills to nurture, to protect, or to maintain their sense of self against subtle, open bias, exclusivity, or rejection. Children must first like, respect, and appreciate themselves before they can do this for another human being.

We need to explore and learn about ourselves. We do this by facing our darkness and our weaknesses; and by working through these aspects of ourselves to draw strength from them. We cannot fully know our strengths until we know our weaknesses. When we know our weaknesses and shortcomings and we use them to grow spiritually, we become messengers for God.

Our self-esteem is the vehicle we use in life to accomplish what we set out to do. It takes you to your destinations throughout your life. It is a multi-layered component of your humanness. To have good self-esteem you must have the same positive feelings for other people that you have for yourself. And when you put positive thoughts into your mind, you get a positive view of yourself, which is your outer, public self-esteem. And when you hold a positive outlook on life, it can be likened to putting premium gas in your car as opposed to regular gas. You can still drive your car; it just does not operate at peak performance. The same is true for your self-esteem. You may like yourself enough to get out of bed to go to work each day. However, if you want a $100 or more pay increase, you will need to improve your self-esteem.

A positive self-esteem brings forth a positive attitude. Your attitude will determine your altitude in life. The attitude you hold about yourself and others will decide whether you go to great heights in life to receive honors and recognition or go downward in life to experience a life of poverty crime, ridicule or imprisonment.

When we have high self-esteem, we show respect for ourselves and others. We are able to listen, reflect on what we hear, and determine if our behavior or actions raise or lower our self-esteem. You will go as far in life as your self-esteem allows. When we have low, or no self-esteem, we dislike ourselves and other people. We are rude, aggressive, rebellious, and defiant. When we have high self-esteem, we show respect for ourselves and others. We have a pleasing disposition, we are tolerant, kind, caring, and a good listener, we have an even temperament and have control over our mouths and control over our emotions.

True personal freedom is your ability to choose your attitude, actions and reactions. When you are in control of yourself, you are free to be your own person, and live your life as you choose. Self-control and self-discipline is the price you pay for freedom. Avoid the tendency to seek a life of ease and comfort, for both lead to decay, poverty, and self-destruction.

If your self-esteem is damaged through generations of abuse, your emotional security is affected. It affects your Self-Identity/Self-Concept, Self-Image, Self-Acceptance, Self-Respect, Self-Worth, and Self-Confidence.

Our sense of Security is provided through our family ties, or roots. Our ancestral family ties provide a point of beginning for us. It answers the questions: "Where did I come from? Who do I belong to? Am I part of a larger network?" This diagram shows the relationship of the child to the family tree.

### Cultural Identity➔ Self-Identity➔ Ethnic Pride➔ Acculturation➔ Assimilation➔ Integration

If a child can identify with this network and find their place, the result can enrich, and give them a sense of empowerment. Family reunions serve this purpose. They bring together generations of ancestors who are talked about and seen in a family portrait album as they come alive and real. The factors that work to give us a sense of importance and security can also negatively affect our self-esteem. Listed are a number of factors that build self-esteem when employed, and tear it down when not employed. These factors are:

1. Culture➔ Self-Identity➔ Ethnic Pride➔ Acculturation➔ Assimilation➔
2. Cultural Values of Acceptable, Appropriate Behaviors
3. Ridicule➔ Embarrassment➔ Shame➔ Low Self-Worth➔ Confusion
4. Self-Limiting Beliefs➔ Thoughts➔ Behavior

**Self Identity** – the self-identity of African Americans has been negatively impacted due to many causes. 1. Past suffering and emotional

101

pain caused by racial discrimination and segregation. 2. Emotional dependency on whites for their sense of identity, to define who they were, whether they and their behaviors were acceptable. There was a strong dependence on whites for their jobs, education, livelihood, and social status. African Americans must stop expecting whites to accept blame for their plight. They must heal the past by acknowledging and accepting the pain and suffering they endured. They cannot afford to wallow in self-pity because it destroys their self-esteem, rather than building self-pride and character.

African Americans have endured verbal, emotional, and physical abuse resulting from covert and overt racism and discrimination in the United States, and experienced physical and emotional trauma.

When asked about suffering, Mother Theresa stated, "Suffering can be a blessing in disguise. I think it is very good when people suffer. To me that is like the kiss of Jesus, and a sign that this person has come close to Jesus, to share this passion ." From a spiritual perspective, suffering has a purpose beneath it. Suffering softens our heart, and opens our awareness to receive God's grace. This is not meant to minimize the atrocity of self-degradation, humiliation, rejection, and the emotional scarring Blacks have endured in their quest to be recognized and accepted as worthwhile human beings and persons of value.

I agree with the statement made by Eleanor Roosevelt, "No one can reject you without your permission." African Americans have given too much value to the opinions of whites, and what they think about them. If you like and accept yourself, it does not matter what whites, or anyone think about you. However, this state of mind is not easy to achieve. We are social beings who want to be accepted by others. You should make an effort to be socially acceptable. However, if you are not accepted, you must acknowledge that you may never get the acceptance you are seeking. People will either like you, or dislike you for their own personal reason, which you may never know. So you have to get on with the task to live your life. There are some things we have to place in God's hand.

African Americans have for too long tried to please whites, to no avail. It is time to Let Go the frustration, and give the problem to God. Your energies can be best used learning about: economics, what you can do to build a strong legacy of love, trust, cooperation, and financial independence, for yourself other African Americans and society at large.

Ethnic Pride – is an important element provided by your cultural group. It gives you a sense of belonging, and acts as a point of reference. It can create a sense of distinction, or be a source of embarrassment and disgrace for you. This is especially true if your family member is a noted gang/drug leader, or is a relative of Dr. Martin Luther King. You can use your ethnic pride as a tool to help you set goals, and feel proud of yourself.

Family celebrations can include yearly family reunions, or even special holidays especially created for African Americans like Kwanzaa. Kwanzaa is a seven day Christmas celebration, which occurs between December 26 and January 1. It was established by Dr. Ron Maulana Karenga, chairman of the Black Studies department at California State University, Long Beach, to help African Americans develop appreciation for the heritage of their African ancestors, honor their elders, foster unity, set-determination, and cooperation in the African American community. Kwanzaa comes from the Swahili phrase "Matuna Ya Kwanzaa," which means "first fruits of the harvest." There are seven principles (nguzo saba) that are celebrated during Kwanzaa, one for each day of the week. On the last day of Kwanzaa, family, and friends are invited to attend Karamu, which mean "feast." Everyone who attends the feast brings food to share with the group. The observance includes exchanging gifts.

**The Seven Basic Symbols are**

| Mazaa | Crops |
| Mkeka | Mat |
| Kinara | Candle holder |

| | |
|---|---|
| Muhindi | Ears of corn |
| Zawadi | Gifts |
| Kikombe cha Umoja | Unity cup |
| Mishumaa Saba | Seven candles |

| **Nguza Saba** | **The Seven Principles** |
|---|---|
| Umoja | Unity |
| Kujichagulia | Self-determination |
| Ujima | Collective work and responsibility |
| Ujimaa | Cooperative economics |
| Nia | Purpose |
| Kuumba | Creativity |
| Jmani | Faith |

Kwanzaa is not a tradition practiced in the mother land of Africa, where all African Americans originated. However, there are other common bonds that unite all persons of African descent, and that is the land itself.

**Acknowledging Your Heritage**: Our culture gives us information about our ancestors; family members, who lived in Africa and were brought to America as slaves. Although Africans were slaves when they arrived in America, they were considered royalty in Africa. According to their tribal traditions they were a King, Queen, Prince, or Princess.

Listed below are countries in Africa. Identify the one you have heard about with a + in the box next to the country's name. If you have visited any country or know someone who has, put a "v" next to it. Then write about the country(ies) that you visited, in the space below.

- [ ] Algeria
- [ ] Angola
- [ ] Benin
- [ ] Botswana
- [ ] Burkina Faso
- [ ] Burundi
- [ ] Cameroon
- [ ] Cape Verde
- [ ] Central African Republic
- [ ] Chad
- [ ] Comorus
- [ ] Cote d`Ivoire
- [ ] Djibouti
- [ ] Democratic Republic of the Congo
- [ ] Egypt
- [ ] Equatorial Guinea
- [ ] Eritrea
- [ ] Ethiopia
- [ ] Gabon
- [ ] Gambia
- [ ] Ghana
- [ ] Guinea
- [ ] Guinea-Bissau
- [ ] Ivory Coast
- [ ] Kenya
- [ ] Lesotho
- [ ] Liberia

- [ ] Libya
- [ ] Madagascar
- [ ] Malagasy Republic
- [ ] Mali
- [ ] Malawi
- [ ] Mauritania
- [ ] Mauritius
- [ ] Morocco
- [ ] Mozambique
- [ ] Namibia
- [ ] Niger
- [ ] Nigeria
- [ ] Republic of Congo
- [ ] Rwanda
- [ ] Sao Tome and Principe
- [ ] Senegal
- [ ] Seychelles
- [ ] Sierra Leone
- [ ] South Africa
- [ ] Swaziland
- [ ] Sudan
- [ ] Tanzania
- [ ] Togo
- [ ] Tunisia
- [ ] Uganda
- [ ] Zambia
- [ ] Zimbabwe

...................................................................................

...................................................................................

...................................................................................

**Finish This Sentence:** My culture gives me information about my ancestors — family members who lived in Africa and were brought to America as slaves. Although Africans were slaves when they arrived in America, most were considered royalty in Africa. According to their tribal traditions they were a King, Queen, Prince or Princess therefore I am Royalty and behave like a Royal person.............................

...............................................................................

**Complete this sentence,** *I am royalty because ...*

...............................................................................

...............................................................................

...............................................................................

Draw a picture of how you would look as a member of an African Royal family.

A form of ethnic pride for Southern African Americans is:
- Respect for elders (their wisdom and advice is sought)
- To not argue (talk back to adults)

List some ethnic values of your family/clan below
- 
- 
- 
- 

**Self-Image** – Is an inner picture of how you see yourself, reflected in behavior. Our self-concept/identity is formed partly from our cultural identity through the morals and values shared with us by elders and the ethnic pride we develop. It creates a sense of belonging. From which we form our self-image.

Since we see from the inside out, we may always have an inaccurate picture of who we are. If any of the parts that formulate our self-images are distorted, our self-images will be distorted. An example of a distorted self-image is someone who weighs ninety pounds, but whose inner mental picture sees a fat person. To change your self-image, it will require you to change your self-concept. And to improve your self-esteem requires you to improve your self-concept/identity, cultural identity, ethnic pride, and self-image. These are key elements of the self-esteem that are essential for good emotional maturity.

What do you consider to be your greatest barrier to your happiness?
.............................................................................

.............................................................................

.............................................................................

.............................................................................

## MY SELF-ESTEEM

Using a scale of 0 through 10 (0 lowest, 5 average, 10 highest) choose the number that indicates how you feel at this moment and the number that indicates how you want to feel in each of the following areas of self-esteem.

| Self-esteem areas | I feel | I want to feel |
|---|---|---|
| Sense of uniqueness | | |
| Sense of belonging | | |
| Sense of power | | |
| Sense of joy | | |
| Sense of wonder | | |
| Sense of integrity | | |
| Sense of mastery | | |
| Sense of purpose | | |

These are the areas of my self-esteem I choose to develop:

.................................................................................

.................................................................................

.................................................................................

.................................................................................

.................................................................................

.................................................................................

## SELF-CONCEPT

1. Self-Concept/Identity – Is it: nice person, poor me, be perfect, (superiority-inferiority complex)? What mask/masks do you wear? How do you see yourself? List below:

2. Using your non-dominant hand, write about your self-concept.

3. Using your non dominant hand, draw a picture of your self-concept.

4. Write one word that describes your self-concept.

5. What self-concept would you write about if you were unhampered, or felt unlimited?

Draw a picture of this person.

OUR PLACE CENTER OF SELF-ESTEEM
School Motto:
Excellence has no fear of observation, so I can do it!

110

### I LOVE MYSELF THE WAY I AM

*I love myself the way I am; there is nothing I need to change.*
*I'll always be the perfect me; there is nothing to rearrange.*
*I'm beautiful and capable of being the best me I can and*
*I love myself just the way I am.*
*I love you just the way you are; there's nothing you need to do.*
*When I feel the love inside myself, it's easy to love you.*
*Behind your fears, your rage and tears, I see your shining star;*
*and I love you just the way you are.*
*I love all the people the way they are because I can clearly see that*
*all the things I judge are done by people just like me.*
*So, till the birth of peace on earth that only love can bring,*
*I'll help it grow by loving everyone.*
*I love myself the way I am, and still I want to grow.*
*But change outside can only come when deep inside I know*
*I'm beautiful and capable of being the best me I can;*
*and I love myself, just the way I am,*
*I love myself, just the way I am.*

– ANON

## BLOCKS TO YOUR SELF-IMAGE AND SELF-ESTEEM

1.  Abuse-emotional/physical affects the total person.
2.  Negative perceptions we hold about ourselves.
3.  Negative perceptions others hold of us; the words they use when they describe us or the way they tease us; the way they treat us.
4.  Mental image you hold of yourself. Is it a nag, complainer, stupid? What masks do you wear? How do you really see yourself? List below:

5. Using your non-dominant hand, write about your self-image.

6. Using your non dominant hand, draw a picture of your self-image.

7. Write one word that describes your self-image.

8. What self-image would you write about if you were satisfied with yourself?

9. Draw a picture of your self-image.

### Magic Within Me

*I have magic within me.*
*I think I can-and I can.*
*I believe-and it happens*
*I create my own future*
    *out of today's thoughts*
    *and today's plans*
    *and today's actions.*
*I control my own future*
*It is created in my mind*
*What great power I have.*
    — -KATHRYN SOUTHWORTH

## Words of Wisdom

*A journey of a thousand miles begins with one step,*
*You must start where you are.*
*To get where you want to go, or*
*To be what you desire, you must create a vision.*
*Elevate your thoughts and mind to that vision,*
*Hold tenaciously to that vision,*
*As night follows day, your dream will one day become real.*
*God is closer to you than the breath you breathe.*
*God is the breath you breathe.*
— REVEREND IDA GREENE

**Through our desires and goals**
**We become motivated to change our life**

TO DISCOVER YOUR TRUE SELF ASK YOURSELF THESE QUESTIONS

1. Who am I?

   I am........................................................................

2. My likes are:                          My dislikes are:

   .............................................          .............................................
   .............................................          .............................................
   .............................................          .............................................
   .............................................          .............................................
   .............................................          .............................................

3. I am good at doing the following:

4. What I really want to do in life is: (write below)

114

5.  What/Who is the most important thing in your life?

6.  What is your ultimate goal in life?

7.  What do you consider most urgent right now?

8.  What has produced the most happiness in your life?

9.  Finish this statement, *As an adult, if I could only do one kind of work in life, it would be ...*

10. Finish this statement, *I am most unhappy when I have to / need to...*

11. Finish this statement, *I am the happiest when I...*

12. Finish this statement, *I am most unhappy at school when I have to ...*

13. Finish this statement, *I am the happiest at school/home when I ...*

## Chapter 5

## Tame the Demon Within
## to Let Your Best Come Forth

FACTORS AFFECTING SELF-ESTEEM IN AFRICAN AMERICAN
ADOLESCENTS

Self-esteem of the African American adolescent has been **negatively affected** by the following:

1. **Worship of sports and sports figures.**
2. **Making idols of entertainment personalities,** while devaluing themselves (which is inconsistent with their religious training in the Ten Commandments).
3. **Lack of emphasis on education.**
4. **Decreased interest in self-reliance** (inequitable job/money distribution).
5. **Hopeless outlook.**
6. **Lack of respect for adults and elders.**
7. **Unwilling to be disciplined or practice self-control.**
8. **Overt expression of anger and aggression.**
9. **Attitude of "Doing my own thing," "What I do is my business,"** without regard for the community, or younger Blacks who see you as someone to emulate.
10. **Allowing the stereotype others give you** to determine how you feel and behave.
11. **Just doing enough to get by.** (This attitude damages your motivation to excel, deprives you of drive needed to exceed your prior performance).
12. **Holding on to old grudges or grievances.**

ADDITIONAL FACTORS AFFECTING AFRICAN AMERICAN ADOLESCENTS

13. **Blaming God/others for your lack of achievement.**
14. **Giving in to feelings of despair/discouragement.**

15. **Maintaining and hold on to an attitude of, "It will never work, so why bother."**
16. **Being lazy,** expecting someone to take care of you.
17. **Feeling you have nothing of value to share with the Black community.**
18. **Failing to do your best at all times.**
19. **Performing below your capability.**
20. **Looking for, or expecting praise for everything you do** (you do well because your African ancestors believe to do less is humiliating).
21. **Allowing others to decide what you will learn**, or how much education you get.
22. **Feeling it is unmanly or "not the Black way to be well educated."**
23. **Believing you exist in isolation,** that what you do only affects you (some young child is watching, wanting to be like you).
24. **If you are a Black male, deciding it is o.k. to have no goals or aspiration to make your life better.**
25. **Relying on a gang to provide protection, or giving you a sense of importance.**
26. **Feeling you cannot learn anything from your parent** or older Black because their ways are outmoded or old fashioned.
27. **Lack of manners**: Remembering to say please, thank you (to show gratitude); to ask "may I have this," "can you do this for me?" "I apologize," "pardon me; I made a mistake," the use of Soft Power Words™ -"would you, could you."
28. **To show respect by**: Allowing the elderly to go before you, being respectful to the elderly, avoiding the use of profanity, or vulgar words in their presence.
29. The use of a title in front of name when addressing adults – Cousin Betty, Cousin Pearlie, Aunt Mary Standberry, Mrs. Bell.
30. It helps your self-esteem when boys/girls treat young ladies/men with respect. Your behavior says to them, "I know you can behave better, and this is what I expect of you."
31. It affects your self-esteem when you say curse words, or derogatory

words to each other like: bitch (a dog in heat), son-of-a-bitch, bastard (born of parents who are unmarried to each other), and other shaming words.

32. To feel no one cares for you. (You are the child of every African and African American person who ever lived. You are cared about and loved more than you will ever know).

African American parents worry today, not so much about what their child will become but, if male, will he live to be an adult? If you are ever corrected by an adult, be thankful they care enough to let you know you are behaving inappropriately or disrespectful. You have a rich African legacy behind you, an African American community that cares about you, and a loving God who expects you to make something of the life given you. I challenge you to rebuild a sense of community, hope, and caring for your fellow man. The motto in the Black community is "Each one, Teach one," Will you be a follower or a leader?

> *Don't walk in front of me – I may not follow.*
> *Don't walk behind me – I may not lead.*
> *Just walk beside me – and be my friend.*
> – ANON

Rituals such as how to treat the elderly, respect, manners, self-discipline, and self-respect identify us with our community, history, tradition, families, and culture. We are not isolated beings. We are a community and family of human beings, whatever affects the one, affects all. We need rules to live by to have a pleasant society. It involves self-control and self-discipline to transition from childhood to adolescence to adulthood. Below are listed the ancient African guidelines.

### THE TRANSITION FROM CHILDHOOD TO ADOLESCENCE

The journey from the innocence of youth to the turbulence of the teens is a time of transition where youths assert their independence from their parents and family. They decide to think for themselves, and take charge of their life. The moment you decide to do as you please, you are no longer a child, but an adult. And all adults take care of themselves. However, if you are in the stage of feeling you want your freedom, but afraid to venture from the nest then you are in that stage of life called adolescence. Here the "American" African, can learn a lot from the traditions handed down by the African culture from the motherland of Africa. However, there are some similarities. For southern African American's age twelve was the time when young girls took on motherly and household duties, and boys were expected to acquire work to have their own spending money.

In the motherland of Africa, a ceremony was held for all boys and girls at age twelve, to help them make the transition from childhood to young adulthood. The youth were taught the necessary skills needed to assume adulthood if necessary. They had to study the twelve values they needed to master in case they got married or became engaged to be married.

### Twelve Values Youth Need to Master as They Pass from Childhood to Adult

1. **Right Action** – The power to choose how you feel and act in any situation you encounter.
2. **Faith and Trust** – You trust yourself, life, and the abundance of all life and God.
3. **Compassion** – Love. Practice giving love and compassion, so that it returns to you.
4. **Self Honor** – Another name for self-respect. You honor and respect yourself by giving respect to others, and being respectful. You do this so that the respect you give is returned to you.
5. **Knowledge** – Intelligence, you will build your personal power by increasing your self-knowledge and life long learning.
6. **Excellence** – You achieve excellence through meaningful work that is intrinsically enriching to you, by your efforts to become a better

person, and by your commitment to excellence in all areas of your life.

7.  **Adaptable** – You expect change and move with it. You make change your friend. An ancient African Proverb is "change is the only constant."

8.  **Responsibility** – You do this by taking command of your attitude, your choices, your behavior and being accountable for them.

9.  **Good Judgment** – Being guided by that which supports, your growth and well-being.

10. **Integrity** – Doing what is right for yourself and others, by walking your talk.

11. **Grace and Objectivity** – To think for yourself, and not be bound by preconceived notions or limitations.

12. **Community** – Contributing to the quality of life in both the African American community, and community of mankind.


We are a society of many cultures and traditions. All cultural values are in place to help us live together in spite of our differences. Our cultural guidelines for living all ve the basic principles of the Ten Commandments given to Moses by God. Even if your ethnicity is not African American, you will find some of your cultural "dos and don'ts" in the Ten Commandments.

If you have faith and belief, God will help you accomplish anything you desire. You are his beloved child. God wants you to succeed, because you will need God's help to achieve total success. God is pleased when his children take the life and talents given them to make something worthwhile from it. True happiness and success can only be found when you are true to yourself and God, such as when you do the best you can each day, and know when you have reached your human limitations and need divine intervention. No one is completely self-sustaining; we are interdependent beings who need the support of others, their love, grace, and support, and divine inspiration that only God can give. God is a living, loving being. God lives through you, God thinks

through you, breathes through you, smiles through you, and interacts
with other human beings through you. Think on these things, God is:

### God Is
*Intelligence, Knowledge, Order,*
*Supply, Health, Life, Truth,*
*Peace, Beauty, Love,*
*Wholeness Understanding*
*God is the breath you take*
— ROBERT A. RUSSELL

### How To Get What You Want In Life
*You Can Have Anything You Want*
*If You Want It Badly Enough.*
*You Can Be Anything You Want To Be,*
*Have, Anything You Set Out To Accomplish*
*If You Will Hold To That Desire*
*With Singleness Of Purpose.*
— ROBERT COLLIER

### Read
*It is the source of knowledge, wisdom, and wealth.*
— IDA GREENE

**THINGS THAT MAY CONCERN AN AFRICAN AMERICAN ADOLESCENT**

1. Identity Issues→ No One to Share Burdens→ Lack of Support→ No Goal to Achieve→ Apathy→Loss of Drive.
   Write about this.

2. Conflicting cultural values of acceptable, appropriate behaviors. Write about this.

3. Ridicule/Embarrassment→ Shame→ Low Sense of Self.
   How does this appear in your life?

4. Do you have negative or defeatist thoughts about yourself? What are they?

5. Would you like to feel wanted, cared about, or important to someone? To whom?

   Why do you feel this way?

6. What feelings do you now use to hide feelings of isolation, loneliness, or make up for friendship?
   Circle feelings you have below, if not listed write it.
   a) Abandoned
   b) Jealous
   c) Envy
   d) Resentment
   e) lonely
   f) Sad
   g) Disappointed

7. We create our tomorrow by what we dream and plan today. Do you have a vision/dream for your life?
   What is your desire or intention for your life?

**Month and year I will achieve my desires:**
   Personal –

   Vocation/College –

   Spiritual/Religious –

   Fun/Social –

## Chapter 6

## What the African American Therapist Can Do to Improve Self-Esteem in the African American Child

The African American culture is unlike any in the world with its strong emphasis on God/Jesus. Uncles, aunts, grandparents, cousins, and concerned neighbors cared for and disciplined children when parents were away. Children were expected to listen and obey any adult who cared enough to correct their behavior when they misbehaved. It was and is still a sign of caring to let a child know they are misbehaving, and you know they can behave better. Adults **who care** are seen as an aunt or uncle or a member of the family.

The African American child expects you to be concerned enough about them to tell them when they are wrong. And they will sometimes misbehave until you have taken a parental role by addressing their misbehavior. You will need to wear two hats; that of therapist and the other as uncle or aunt. The child expects you to function in this role. They want, need and expect you to take charge and be in command. If you fail to take the lead, they will take it. Because they care about you, they will listen to what you say. Because you are African American, they will listen to you and do as you say. They will not do this for a non African American, because of trust issues.

African Americans have been betrayed and hurt by people who misjudged them, their behavior, or expected the worst outcome for them. They expect you to tell them the truth in a kind and caring way. You can confront them about anything but you must first establish the **caring, trusting** uncle or aunt relationship. Relatives tell you about yourself in a caring way. This is not a fake, phony, *I care about you*. If the words do not match the behavior, you will be treated as any white person, or persons they believe do not care. Your caring has to be genuine. It is not a cold, impersonal detachment. It is a warm caring feeling of "I have been there." They can sense rejection a mile away, because this is what

125

they have experienced most of their life. And even though you are Black like them, you may still be tested. They want to know, "if I am my very worst, will you still like me." If you care, you will hang in there, and still love them while they are learning to trust you.

You cannot be the traditional therapist you were trained to be with the Black/African American counseling client. Your psychological training did not prepare you to counsel the African American client. The academic system you learned works well with the Caucasian client. You will fail miserably if you use the same approach without modification for your Black clients. This client is an "intuitive, feeling" person.

The African American therapist and non-African American need to accept that the paranoia Blacks have towards whites and the establishment is legitimate. This needs to be acknowledged and ways sought to help them deal with this. African Americans need a little healthy paranoia to survive as a race. My mother told me repeatedly, "Remember, Ida, not everyone who smiles and grins in your face is your friend."

The African American therapist must be aware that the existence of Blacks as a race of people in the United States has hinged on their faith in Jesus to bring forth justice on their behalf, that they would one day be accepted by society. The Black church has always told its congregation, "Not to hate those who abuse you, but instead pray for them. If they strike you on one cheek turn the other one to them, for you are as well as them working on your soul's salvation." My mother was steeped in the sayings of Africa. Some of her admonitions to me were: "You can catch more flies with honey than you can with vinegar," (be nice to people), "What goes around, comes around," (whatever people do to you will return to them from someone else), "You have to feed some people with a long handle spoon," (you have to keep your distance with some people), "Don't let your right hand know what your left hand is doing," (don't tell people everything you are thinking; especially if what you want to do or have, seems impossible.)
God never laughs at your weird ideas.

Both the African American and non-African American therapist need to help Blacks acknowledge and cope with the anger and rage they may have (which is legitimate) because of the racism and discrimination they have endured. I had an understanding, kind, Caucasian professor, Dr. I. N. McCollum in the Psychology department at San Diego State University who helped me vent my frustration and hostilities of the past. He was intuitive enough to see that I was acting inferior, and I had untapped potential inside. He helped me with my research to develop the Allport Vernon, Lindsay Test of Values for African Americans. We could not find anyone to publish the test in 1970, so it is in a box in my garage. I may not have helped my people as I had hoped, but it built my self-esteem and confidence to know I was a research scientist who developed a major personality test. Sometimes the roads of life can be rugged.

### The Rugged Roads of Life

*Life is an ever increasing spiral*
*on the path to human perfection.*
*It matters not the hue of your skin,*
*the color of your eyes, nor the color of your hair.*
*For self-mastery is an inner process,*
*that happens each time you overcome an obstacle.*
*No one can ever determine the depth of your learning experience.*
*So continue on your journey, to overcome your stiffest challenges,*
*For no one will ever know, the depths of your overcoming.*
*Continue to strive for excellence in every thing you do.*
*For the path to fulfillment and happiness*
*are the rugged roads of life.*
— IDA GREENE

*A bitter heart devours its owner*
Traditional Sayings of African Peoples
HERERO

127

To work effectively with the African American child, the therapist must keep in mind three factors that dominate the emotional make up of the African American community:

1. God/Jesus is the healing balm that soothes frayed nerves, changes the heart of the unkind slave master, and helps them cope with any problem.
2. The culture operates on a caring, trusting, extended family model, where the words people say are expected to match their body language.
3. Trust is critical, and it operates on an instinctive intuitive basis.

I teach a twelve-week, self-esteem class for African American students, coping with identity issues, behavior management problems or low self-worth. In one class, I gave the students four shapes: square, circle, triangle, squiggly, (wiggly shaped) and asked them to identify with a symbol. 90 percent of the class saw themselves as squiggly. They were told later what the personality characteristics of each represented. The squares are organizers who plan things in advance, (mathematicians, scientists), circles are concerned about relationships-things working well together (teachers), triangles likes order and structure (accountants), and squiggles are creative, intuitive (musicians, artists, orally expressive).

Because of this mini survey, it was apparent to me that there were some cultural similarities. I wanted to be sure they accessed all areas of their brain, and utilized the seven kinds of intelligence that Thomas Armstrong mentions in his book, *7 Kinds of Smarts*. He states, there are many ways to show intelligence.

**The 7 Kinds of Intelligence are:**

1. Linguistic, the intelligence of words, this person can argue, persuade, or instruct through the spoken word.
2. Logical-Mathematical, the intelligence of numbers and logic, is the scientist, accountant, and computer programmer,

3. Spatial Intelligence involves thinking in pictures and images, the ability to perceive, transform and re-create different aspects of the visual spatial world (architects, pilots and mechanical engineers).

4. Bodily-Kinesthetic Intelligence of the physical self-includes talent in controlling one's body movements and handling objects skillfully (athletes, mechanics, and surgeons).

5. Musical Intelligence is the capacity to perceive, appreciate and produce rhythms and melodies.

6. Interpersonal Intelligence is the ability to understand and work with other people (Dr. Martin Luther King Jr., negotiators, teachers).

7. Intrapersonal is intelligence, of the inner self. A person strong in this kind of smart can easily access her own feelings, discriminate between many different kinds of inner emotional states and use her self-understanding to guide her life. Examples of these individuals are counselors, theologians, self-employed business persons.

Mr. Armstrong develops each of these intelligences in his book, and gives excellent example of how to implement each. It would be wise for anyone who teaches African American children to be aware of the information in the book *7 **Kinds of Smarts***.

The conditions of the learning environment must be conducive to learning, to maximize the learning experience for the African American child, and are listed below:

LEARNING ENVIRONMENT CONDITIONS THAT FOSTER LEARNING
1. Positive attitude
2. Concentration
3. Being focused (focusing of the eye span)
4. Erect posture
5. Excitement for learning
6. Desire to be a better person
7. Drive to know or learn more
8. Have a love or passion for reading

Which of the above principles do you have, or now use at school or home? Write your thoughts or feelings about this now.

## LEARNING STYLES INVENTORY

All children perceive the world in a different way, therefore they learn differently. Many are visual (sight) learners, others learn by auditory (hearing), while others learn or experience the world through kinesthetic (touch) sensation. Go through the statements below; decide if the statement refers to someone who is a visual, auditory, or kinesthetic (touch) learner. Write A, V, or K beside the statement. Then write the word 'me' by every statement that applies to you. Tally your responses to find the dominant channel you use to learn or express yourself.

1.  I like to work in a group because I learn from the others in my group. ☐
2.  When the teacher says a number, I don't understand it until I see it written. ☐
3.  Writing a spelling word down several times helps me remember it better. ☐
4.  I find it easier to remember what I have heard than what I have read. ☐
5.  I learn best when I study alone. ☐
6.  I like to listen to music or television when I study. ☐
7.  If I have a choice between reading and listening, I usually listen. ☐
8.  I talk better than I write. ☐
9.  I use my hands a lot when I talk. ☐
10. When I am told the pages of my homework, I can remember them without writing them down. ☐
11. I can get more school work done when I work with someone. ☐
12. Written math problems are easier for me to do than oral. ☐

13. If my home work were verbal, I would do it faster. ☐
14. I study best when no one is around to talk or listen to. ☐
15. I do best in classes where the information has to be read. ☐
16. I like to do things with my hands, like crafts or simple repairs. ☐
17. The things I write on paper seem better when I say them. ☐
18. Written assignments are easier for me. ☐
19. I understand a math problem that is written better than one I hear. ☐
20. I like to work by myself. ☐
21. I would rather read a story, than listen to it read by someone. ☐
22. I would rather show and explain how a thing works than write about it. ☐
23. Saying my multiplication tables over and over helps me remember them better than to write them over and over. ☐
24. I learn better by listening than by reading. ☐
25. I like to make things with my hands. ☐
26. I do well on tests if they are about things I hear in class. ☐
27. It is easier when I say the numbers of a problem to myself as I work it out. ☐
28. I like to study with other people. ☐
29. I like tests that call for sentence completion or written answers. ☐
30. I would rather tell a story than write about it. ☐

## To Tally Your Score -

Remember there is no right or wrong answer. You are trying to discover how you perceive and interact with your environment. Give yourself one point for each answer you mark 'me' against each of A, V or K. Your highest score is your dominant sensory channel, your next highest and so forth.

Write your observations and thoughts below.

## How to make a Therapeutic Intervention with an Attention Deficit Child

In my private practice over fifteen years treating children with Attention Deficit Disorder, I found three behavioral therapeutic interventions that worked. The Attention Deficit Disorder (ADD) child or Hyperactive Disorder child is unable to handle multiple stimuli. So the goal is to reduce or minimize incoming stimuli or information. The following suggestions are offered to work with the ADD child, so they can manage themselves.

1. Speak Slowly
2. Reduce external stimulation as much as possible
3. Make direct eye contact when speaking to the child
4. Repeat verbal information for reinforcement
5. Allow the child an opportunity to utilize diversified classroom activities such as; puzzles, drawing, cutting out pictures. Change the activity or environment often for variety and maintain the child's interest.

Attention deficit children have difficulty listening to cerebral stimuli, to follow a command. This is a two step behavioral process that is easy for the average child. However, an add child is bombarded continuously with a barrage of internal stimuli, so they are highly stimulated. If you can reduce the stimulation outside their mind, to help them relax, you will have a better chance of making a positive therapeutic intervention with them.

1. The child with a *low attention span requires physical and verbal reinforcement*; to get them to listen and follow a simple command, like sit down. It may be necessary to gently help them start the sitting activity, while you speak what you want them to do. Example, "David let's sit in the chair now". First show them what you want them to do and then help them do it, without being forceful.
2. For the child with a *moderate attention span*, repeat *the command in a stern tone of voice, slowly, until the child hears it*, and is able to follow the command.

3. If the child has a *high attention span, repeat the command three times while you make eye contact.* If you do not get the results you desire, resort to level 2 commands.

The African American therapist must never buy into the belief of them being overly involved with the African American client. You make your connection and relevance with this client, through involvement. The culture you deal with is engaging and interactive; it operates on a personal relationship basis. Your effectiveness is in your ability to become an extended family member. If you are perceived as cold, detached, and uncaring, you may not be able to connect with the African American client. If you do not respect your client, or you look on them with disgust, or sympathy they will sense it. You will be perceived as an outsider, someone who is "Black on the outside and white on the inside." This means you are black, but think or act from a white frame of reference. You may have good intentions, but if what you want to share does not fit into the mind set of the African American clients, they will not reveal themselves to you completely.

Because of the strong religious background of most Blacks, that emphasizes the love and caring nature of Jesus, many Blacks expect other Blacks to be caring, compassionate and understanding. If your behavior is different, you will be viewed with a jaundiced eye and your motives will be questioned. Even as an African American therapist, when you match the cultural thoughts of the client, you may still have to prove or show how much you care. If so it will take you a longer time to establish a bond, but once you do, you will be able to move the client quickly to a therapeutic outcome. So it is worth the bother. The African American client is worth the bother, and you are worth the bother.

Many children with Attention Deficit Disorder can benefit from activities that help them use their critical thinking skills. The exercise below can help you engage the African American child in a mutually satisfying activity that is fun.

1. Solve these problems using both divergent (separating the parts) and convergent (combine similar patterns) thinking. Take one minute for each exercise. Increase your time by one minute if needed. Create other whole brain exercises of your own also.

   a. taepitn

   b. pilnec

   c. pyahp

2. Connect all nine dots without taking your pencil off the paper.

3. Now you create something, a poem, melody etc.

The answers to #1 exercise above are: patient, pencil, happy.

In addition the African American therapist needs to be aware that Blacks are experiencing a Post Traumatic Stress Syndrome, exhibited in their sense of apathy, diminished energy, low drive, and fear to actively engage themselves and participate fully in a government and society that has never accepted them. This is why many Blacks feel they are entitled to the 20 acres and a mule once promised to them by the Federal Government.

Blacks have been misled, discounted, and assumed stupid by persons who do not understand their humble and gentle ways. The culture of the African American emphasizes respect for elders. Its deeply religious upbringing reinforces the principle that Jesus taught that is we can not enter the kingdom of God unless we become as little children. You may not see this behavior in urban African American children, but it is prevalent in African Americans over thirty, or those who live in the south.

Dr. Martin Luther King Jr. stated in *Ebony,* January 1958, "we must teach every Negro child that rejection of heritage means loss of cultural roots, and {that} people who have no past have no future. The content of one's character is the important thing, not the color of the skin."

### CULTURAL SIMILARITIES

While there are many differences that distinguish the African American from other cultures and society at large, there are many similarities that unite them with all people. Some cultural similarities that all people of the human race feel are:

Hurt
Sadness
Loneliness
Pain
Anger
Fear
Joy
Love

Can you think of other similarities? Write them below.

## Valuing Our Differences

Diversity is anything that distinguishes us or divides us from another ethnic culture or group of people. Our differences are to be understood and celebrated. Our culture can act as a bridge to bring us together as a member of the family of mankind.

## Cultural Differences
### Communication
Language (dialect)

### The way you process (receive) information
1. Auditory 2. Visual 3. Kinesthetic

Body language

Language you speak other than English?

List below other languages you speak or write:

### Ethnicity:
American Indian/Alaskan Islander
Asian/Pacific Islander
Black/African American
Filipino
Hispanic
White/Caucasian
Other/Africans, Panamanian, Samoan
Puerto Rican,

If your ethnic identity is not listed, please write it down...

Are you happy with your ethnicity?
If your answer is **no**, state why below

**Gender:**
Female
Male
Persons who want/feel their biological sex is not how they feel

**Religious Differences**
Protestant – (Jesus is Christ, Savior of mankind)

Catholic – (Belief in Trinity, Pope is the intermediary between God and man)

New Thought – (Metaphysical, looks for the implied spiritual meaning in the Bible.)

Unity – (Practical approach to religion "God loves us unconditionally")

Religious Science – (Scientific approach to religion; "heal the mind of error thoughts, we are one with the mind of God.")

Christian Scientist – (Do not believe in medicine or medical treatment)

Jehovah Witness – (Does not accept Jesus as Christ; does not receive blood if sick)

137

Essene – (Old religion, they say "Jesus was an Essene"; focus on nature, eat raw vegetables to purify body, no meat)

Buddhist – (Use the word "Buddha" instead of "God" [see Jesus as a wise teacher])

Jewish – (Do not believe in Jesus/New Testament)

Mohammed – (Allah is God, sees Jesus as a wise man)

Agnostic – (There is no God)

Atheist – (Orderly causation)

**Political Orientation Differences**
Money is seen as an ends to a means or as power.
One is not worthwhile if they cannot provide for themselves.

**Values that can be culturally different are:**
Cleanliness, work, family size, leisure activities, time, play
Music – Country Western, Rhythm and Blues
Humor – (quick witted, story telling)

**Ways to communicate with others from a different cultural background**
  a. Listen with intent to hear
  b. Speak slowly
  c. Repeat statement to make sure you are heard
  d. Maintain eye contact without staring
  e. Accept the differences
  f. Practice patience
  g. Expect to learn something new

Reverend David Spears states, that "our differences are to be accepted and celebrated".

*Write down any differences you have come to accept rather than fear.*

SKILLS FOR SPEAKING
## Use I-messages when speaking.

An I-message is a sentence that starts with the word 'I' and expresses a feeling.

Be aware and always state what you are feeling.

The Four Basic Feelings are:
1. **Mad**
2. **Sad**
3. **Glad**
4. **Fear/afraid.**

## Other useful feeling words are:

I like it when...          I want...
I don't like it when...    I wish...

*It is the rainy season that gives wealth.*
Traditional Sayings of African Peoples
HAUSA

FACTORS THAT PROMOTE OPEN COMMUNICATION

## Dos and Don'ts to listen effectively

**Do** remember that every person has the right to any feeling in the world.

**Do** know that people do not have to agree with you or you with them for things to be o.k.

**Do** put your feelings "on a back burner" (lay your feelings aside) while you are the listener.

**Don't** say or imply that the person "shouldn't feel that way."

**Don't** express your feelings—of disagreement, when the other person is upset.

**Don't** interpret what you think the other person really feels.

**Don't** try to get the person to change their mind when they have voiced their concern or stated their position.

FACTORS THAT ENSURE OPEN COMMUNICATION

A. Flexible attitude

B. Openness to change

C. Willingness to learn something new

D. Tolerance for ambiguity

E. Open-mindedness

# Chapter 7

## Agony and Ecstasy of the Evolving Self

If you desire improvement of your self-esteem you will need to change the way you currently think, define, and see yourself and, also, the way you behave. The key word here is change. There is a lot of changing you will need to do. If you are unwilling, toss this book in the trash can, or tear it up now! If you are willing to take a small step towards improving yourself, I applaud you! It takes courage and self-love to look at oneself objectively with the intention to be a better person.

If you are unhappy with yourself or your life you must take corrective action. This is a do-it-yourself task. No one can do it for you. No one knows your likes and dislikes. No one, but you and God, knows you intimately. And God knows you better than you know yourself. God knows who you are (his child), God knows who and what you are capable of being. God does not put limitations on your ability or potential. God always say "Yes," to anything you want in life. The critical factors are that; you want this with all your mind, body, and soul, you are willing to pay whatever price necessary to get what you want, you are unwavering in your desire or quest to have what you want, and most important is – that it does not infringe upon the rights of your fellow human beings, and what you want is for the good of all people every where. Most of us keep our longings and desires to ourselves, and never share them with others. If others do not know what we want, they do not know how to help us.

Your mind is not open for all to see; others cannot read your mind. You are the only person who knows the thoughts that go through your mind. This is your uniqueness. This is how you differ from others, and they from you. This is the grand design behind individuality. This is why it is futile to compare yourself with another, or try to live your life as another person lives.

There are many change events happening in the lives of African Americans; a blurred self-identity; an increase in crime in the black community; the disappearance of affirmative action; the emergence of aids among the heterosexual population; gang related crime; drive-by shootings; the million man march with black men saying they will be responsible for the children they father; the acknowledgement of Jesus by Muslims; the emergence of skin heads and hate militia; the prevalence of rap music; the foul and vulgar language of rap and other music; the decline in church attendance (due to work schedules, football, basketball, and other non-church activities like Saturday night concerts); increase in alcohol and drug use. All these events might give the impression the African American family is disintegrating. However, the Black community is rediscovering itself. It now realizes it had greatness, togetherness, a respect and love for each other it took for granted.

Dr. Martin Luther King commented, when asked about crime in the Black community, "The Negro is not criminal by nature. Criminality is environmental, not racial. Poverty and ignorance breed crime whatever the racial group may be. We must work to remove the system of segregation, discrimination and the existence of economic injustice if we are to solve the problem of crime in the Negro community."

The recent alarming data shows that welfare pays more than most jobs. Work allows you to gain self-pride and self-respect. This is something you cannot have with free money. Whatever anyone gives you, you pay for with a loss of self-pride and self-respect. Welfare is alright if it is short term (say, 1–2 years) until you get on your feet. However, anything over that destroys your self-respect, and self-pride. It is better to earn a small amount of money and be proud of of it, rather than having a large sum of money that is given to you. This obligates you, takes your initiative, and self-determination to better your life and affairs. Welfare erodes your self-confidence and belief in your ability to be self-sufficient. We all need help sometimes. My family was on welfare for one year when I was a teenager, and I was glad when we got off it. During that time our household began to deteriorate, and I was ashamed that we were on welfare. I started baby-sitting to earn spending money; we could keep the money as long as our school work was done, and our grades were maintained above a "C."

Our self-respect and self-pride cannot be bought. We get it through what we do with our life. We must be careful to act, behave and live from the premise that God is sufficient to supply our needs, as did our ancestors years ago. When you become dependent on anything or anyone to supply your needs, the person or thing has the power to make you sad or glad. You lose control over yourself and affairs. Then your self-esteem, self-respect, and self-confidence suffer.

On self-confidence, Dr. Martin Luther King Jr. wrote the following comments, in *Ebony*, January 1958 issue, "1. Know yourself, analyze yourself and discover your potentialities as well as your limitations. 2. Accept yourself; never try to be anybody else. Realize that you have something unique to offer society, however humble it is. 3. Trust yourself. In spite of the limitations you may have. Never develop an inferiority complex. Always develop an internal sense of security that no external situation can remove. 4. Deny yourself. You lose confidence in yourself when you think too much about yourself. Nine times out of ten, people are not thinking about you."

There are two sources of confidence, yourself and other people. Self-approval from within gives you feelings of accomplishment, self-worth, and self-identity. It is the belief in yourself, and feeling capable. To know you are doing your best, liking yourself, and feeling you can do what you desire. Self-confidence from the outside is dependent upon other's approval, winning their acceptance, respect, and recognition. On the outside, self-confidence is being important, needed, including a pat on the back, and being asked to join things. Problems with self-confidence arise when there is a gap between how you feel about yourself in the present, how you would like to feel, or how people see you now, and how you would like them to see you.

Challenge is what life is about. Strive to do your life's work as if God called you to do it. Do it with a sense of divine responsibility, no matter how insignificant it may be. In the words of Dr. Martin Luther King Jr. "Do a little job in a big way and an ordinary job in an extraordinary way. If you can't be a pine on the top of a hill, be a scrub in the valley, but be the best little scrub on the side of the hill. Be a bush if you can't be a tree. If you can't be the sun, be a star. For it isn't by the size that you win or fail. Be the best of whatever you are. If it falls your lot to sweep streets, sweep them like Michelangelo painted pictures, like Shakespeare wrote poetry, like Beethoven composed music."

African Americans must refocus their energy on education and economics, as in the past. Dr. King feels "the function of education is to teach one to think intensively and critically. We must remember that intelligence is not enough? Intelligence plus character is the true goal of education." In Ebony, July 1956, he had this to say, "On Economic Emancipation, Negroes must learn to practice systematic saving. They must also pool their economic resources through various cooperative enterprises, such as credit unions, savings bonds, and finance companies." Today Blacks can buy mutual funds, money market funds, long term Ginnie Mae bonds, invest in the stock market, buy a Keogh Retirement Plan, 401K retirement plan, tax deferred annuities, buy a ten-year paid-up life insurance policy, or other methods to financially prepare for retirement. We must do the best we can with the talents and resources (our minds) God has given us. For we are God's gift to us, what we make of ourselves is our gift to God. Will you return to God a masterpiece worth beholding, or the heap of ashes from which you came?

Each of us is here by divine appointment. Each has a different task to complete for our journey on earth. Each has a different mission and purpose to be alive. No two are alike. Share your dreams, visions, sorrows and accomplishment with others. You may give them an idea on how to best proceed at a task, but remember it must be done in their special way, not your way.

Work to improve your relationship with yourself, and then with others. Your relationship with others provides the refinement you need as a human being. **Here are some guidelines on friendship and how to be a good friend.**

1. **When someone entrusts you** with their inner possessions, thoughts and feelings, be a good steward of them.
2. **To be a good steward,** honor the trust placed in you in best way you can.
3. **Trust is not easy to give**. It takes time, and the development of confidence to share oneself with another.
4. **Trust and rely on letting go**, to rely on another person' judgment.
5. **When someone trusts you,** they are reaching out in faith – you should be honored.
6. **Respect the confidence others place in you** to share their personal/private self.
7. **Recognize others are reaching out to you**; welcome this open and honest communication.
8. **Act as a good steward** of the innermost thoughts and feelings shared with you.
9. **Be considerate**; conscious of your thoughts when dealing with others; aware of your actions and words.
10. **Give thanks for the wisdom of God** that helps you to be a good confidant, and steward of another's private space.

Each of us has shortcomings. You were given a body by God. You chose and were afforded the privilege by God/Jesus to have an earth experience to work on your soul imperfections. This is done through your relationships, and encounters with others, who are also here to complete the lessons they need to learn. It is a privilege and blessing to be alive. Appreciate all relationships. You learn from the good as well as bad ones. Try to harmonize your relationships with others.

TO HARMONIZE YOUR RELATIONSHIPS WITH OTHERS

1. Do not demean or ridicule another person.
2. Do not challenge another.
3. Respect disagreement.

145

4. Do not treat anyone in a condescending way.
5. Do not speak for others.
6. Don't interrupt when another person is speaking.
7. Do not think someone is exceptional or special.
8. Notice what you expect from others.
9. Know that others may not always speak on the present issues.
10. Do not assume everyone will do what you expect.

### How to help others get a larger view of themselves

This exercise is a group project. Form a group of five persons. Each person is asked to describe themselves to the group. As each group member describes themselves, make notes of each person's strengths, favorable characteristics they may have overlooked or not emphasized strongly. Take turns telling each person about your observations.

1. Group member's name: ...........................................
The favorable ways you impressed me were

..........................................................................

..........................................................................

..........................................................................

2. Group member's name: ...........................................
The favorable ways you impressed me were

..........................................................................

..........................................................................

..........................................................................

146

3. Group member's name: ..........................................

The favorable ways you impressed me were

...............................................................

...............................................................

...............................................................

4. Group member's name: ..........................................

The favorable ways you impressed me were

...............................................................

...............................................................

...............................................................

5. Group member's name: ..........................................

The favorable ways you impressed me were

...............................................................

...............................................................

...............................................................

*The only way to have a friend is to be one.*
– RALPH WALDO EMERSON

## IMAGES OF YOU

If a child believes s/he will lose important relationships if s/he fails to meet others needs or, or if s/he is different from others, s/he will develop a "public self" different from the "private self" s/he is inside.

Circle the words you think describes how other people perceive you now. Then put a box around the words you believe portray how you reality are.

| Others Perception | | Your Perception | |
|---|---|---|---|
| Happy | Distant | Anxious | Angry |
| Inferior | Handsome | Inferior | Warm |
| Intelligent | Skinny | Scared | Kind |
| Handsome | Friendly | Confident | Skinny |
| Secure | Scared | Tense | Considerate |
| Attractive | Caring | Patience | Anxious |
| Dumb | Shy | Sad | Quiet |
| Caring | Mean | Sensitive | Shy |
| Fat | Distant | Lonely | Insecure |
| Talkative | Gossip | Lonely | Scared |

## NEEDED: MORE WINNERS

| Winners | Losers |
|---|---|
| The winner dares to be different. | The loser resists change. |
| *The winner expects the best.* | *The loser believes the worst.* |
| The winner has a compelling purpose | The loser has convenient excuses. |

| Winners | Losers |
|:---:|:---:|
| *The winner is confident of victory.* | *The loser fears. failure* |
| The winner is a dynamic part of the answer | The loser is part of the problem |
| *The winner lives from well-springs of faith.* | *The loser exists in cesspools of doubt.* |
| The winner is motivated by self determined goals. | The loser is limited by self-imposed boundaries. |
| *The winner grows gracious in the garden of gratitude.* | *The loser struggles in cobweb of complaints.* |
| The winner becomes vitalized. | The loser is victimized. |
| *A winner is excited by  challenges.* | *The loser is controlled by obstacles.* |
| The winner is propelled by possibilities. | The loser is perplexed by problems. |
| *The winner creates opportunities* | *The loser magnifies misfortunes.* |
| The winner is original. | A loser loves conformity. |
| *The winner is activated by adventure* | *The loser is constricted by caution.* |
| The winner grows up, looks up, and steps up. | The loser gives up. |

# Chapter 8

## Abuse — Its Effect upon the Total Person

Emotional abuse affects our sense of self and self-esteem. An assault to our emotional health is as equally devastating as sexual or physical abuse. It is an injury to the core of one's personality.

African Americans are still suffering from, and acting out, the abuse inflicted upon them generations ago. You must be aware of this to insure you do not inflict the abuse you encountered and endured on your fellow African Americans. This awareness, acknowledgement and acceptance are critical. For we can cannot avoid doing something we do not consider a problem. We pass on to the next generation our life experiences.

Bad things do happen to good people. It is not what happens to you that matters, but how you feel, and react to what has happened to you. You can let a bad experience transform you, so you help others in a similar situation and you can live peacefully with yourself and others, or you can become bitter, angry, rebellious, defiant, militant, unable to cope with life, or you can work to forgive those who abused you.

You have a rich heritage on how to survive and overcome adversity. If you are reading this book you are a survivor. Many people both White and Black died that you might be free to express your individuality and creativity (John F. Kennedy, Bobby Kennedy, Medgar Evers, Dr. Martin Luther King and others). You have an obligation to help the next generation. Man's inhumanity to each other can end with you. What can you do to end prejudice, hatred, bigotry and violence?

Abuse means mistreating another person. Abuse may be physical, emotional, or sexual. The word "abuse" can be used to mean each of these, or it can be used to mean all three of them. The term "domestic violence," when used refers to physical abuse or "battering." Battering or "wife-beating" is the term often used to identify abuse by a man against a woman; however, a man may also be abused. Statistics show that 95-97% of battering is men against women.

Until recently, many people thought men had a right to batter their women. Wife beating was even protected by law. In 1824 the Supreme Court of Mississippi ruled that a husband should be allowed to chastise without being subject to vexatious prosecution, which would supposedly shame all parties. In 1964, a North Carolina court ruling asserted that the state should not interfere in cases of domestic chastisement but should leave the parties to themselves, to make up, unless there were permanent injuries or an excess of violence. In many countries outside the United States, a woman is still considered the property of her husband. In medieval Europe 476-1453 A.D. feudal law made wives their husbands' chattel – with wifely disobedience enforced by community punishments such as iron muzzles with spikes that depressed the tongue.

In the United States, "wife-beating," became illegal early last century, but it continues even to today though it is illegal. Learned behavior patterns are not as easy to change as is a law. Battering, "wife beating," continues to make the news; however, sexual abuse and emotional abuse is rarely addressed. Sexual abuse tends to be associated with children. On the other hand, emotional abuse is rarely addressed as a problem, and it is the most insidious of all. Emotional abuse is mistreating and controlling another through their feelings. It erodes a person's belief in themself; it is subtle and is often stated as verbal ribbing that hurts through callous words, poor word choice, or lack of concern for the other. Most of us abuse ourselves and others on a daily basis because we have not been sensitized to the painful effects of emotional trauma.

Abused people can suffer Post Traumatic Stress Disorder, which is not unlike concentration camp victims or earthquake victims. The American Psychiatric Association gives this definition of Post Traumatic Stress Disorder (DSM-111-R): ***The person has experienced an event that is*** *outside the range of usual experience that would be markedly distressing to almost anyone, e.g. serious threat or harm to one's children, spouse or other close relative.*

We are a tapestry of many splendid textures. There is one God who made all. You are one of God's special children. I believe in you. You are enough. You do not need to do or be more to receive love. You have been blessed immensely. Start now to count your blessings. You are a multi-talented creation. What will you give back to the world? Your sole purpose for existing is to discover and know yourself. Know your strengths, limitations, your weakness, and the gift you are to share with the world. You are a gift to the world, and you have a gift to share with mankind.

### WAYS YOU MAINTAIN LOW SELF-ESTEEM

**You lower your self-esteem by:**

- ☐ Depending upon others for a sense of importance.
- ☐ Not accepting complete responsibility for your life.
- ☐ Depending upon others to do what you need to do.
- ☐ Not setting clear goals.
- ☐ Depending upon others permission before I am able to act.
- ☐ Not differentiating between who you are and what you do.
- ☐ Comparing yourself to others, to make them a
- ☐ Thinking your decisions need to be perfect or right.
- ☐ Failing to make choices, or think in a rigid/limited manner.
- ☐ Not giving yourself permission to make a mistake or fail.
- ☐ Not allowing yourself freedom to express your thoughts or feelings.
- ☐ Being fearful and anxious about things you can do nothing about.
- ☐ Thinking another person's brain is better equipped to solve your problems.
- ☐ Thinking you need to be perfect, to be o.k.
- ☐ Being afraid to step outside your comfort zone; overly self-conscious.

Check the ones above that apply to you, then state why this is an issue.

..............................................................................

..............................................................................

..............................................................................

## SELF-DESCRIPTION
### Answer these Questions for Yourself
Who am I? What am I like? How do others see? What are my strengths?
What are areas of my life I want to develop great skills in? Write a description of what you are like. This exercise will increase your self-awareness and self-disclose skills. Sit down now, summarize what you have learned about yourself.

1

..............................................................................

..............................................................................

..............................................................................

2.

..............................................................................

..............................................................................

..............................................................................

3.

..............................................................................

..............................................................................

..............................................................................

**WAYS TO CHANGE A LOW SELF-IMAGE**

1. Change all negative images you hold about yourself to positive.

2. Do you have negative thoughts, or feelings towards anyone? Why? Who is it?

3. What can you do to heal this/these relationship/s?

4. To know what you feel, write what you are feeling right now.

5. To cope with feeling of being unloved, list the names of anyone who has ever shown you tenderness or affection.

**Change your thinking to *Light The Fire Within You*™**

# THINGS I WILL CHANGE AS OF TODAY

*I now affirm that:*
*I like me.*
*I like the person I am becoming.*
*I trust my judgment.*
*I trust my decision making ability.*
*I know my mind is good as that of any other person.*
*I accept that my mind will work for me.*
*I know I can make wise decisions.*
*I have an excellent memory.*
*I can depend on my mind to remember things.*
*I can figure things out with my keen, sharp, mind.*
*I now release anger, resentment, and all past
    unhappy thoughts.*
*It is O.K. for me to make a mistake.*
*It is O.K. for me to not be perfect.*
*It is O.K. for me to relax.*
*It is O.K. for me to be me.*
*It is O.K. for me to not know everything.*
*It is O.K. for me to be corrected or receive input
    about myself.*
*It is O.K. for me to enjoy life.*

— IDA GREENE

# Chapter 9

## Healing the Shattered Self-Image —
## How to set Boundaries for Yourself

Remember who you are. You are a product of the wisdom, knowledge, genius, and prophetic powers of your ancestors, and people who lived before you. Who you are is God's gift to you. What you make of yourself is your gift to God. Will you give back to God the lump of clay from which you came? Or will your life be a masterpiece to behold? The answer is inside you. You hold the key to your future. You decide your destiny. God has given you freedom of choice, and Jesus is only a prayer away. You can make a difference. You matter; you are special. You have inside you all the talent of the ages. Walk tall and proudly. You are somebody. You are you and that is enough.

1. **Accept that you are important to life**.
2. **Accept that you are valued by God**; therefore you have self-worth, self-value, and importance.
3. **Accept that all people are special** including you.
4. **Respect your right to privacy as well as the rights of others.**
5. **Accept that no one is here to satisfy your needs** and neither are you here to meet the needs of others.
6. **Accept that others have to want to love us,** and care about/care for us. We can not demand that others love us. It is their choice to like or love us. And we let it be o.k.
7. **If we have abused others verbally,** emotionally or physically, they will be afraid to trust us, because they fear being hurt by us again.
8. **We have to earn others' trust, love, and affection,** it is not a right or privilege they owe us.
9. **Tell the truth,** never say "it does not matter," when it does.
10. **Accept your feelings**. Acknowledge your pain, hurt, disappointment, depression, grief, feelings of: sadness, rejection, loneliness,

abandonment, resentment, anger, rage, and lack of love.

11. **To have love you must be love and express love,** to attract love into your life. So daily send love to yourself and others. Send love to others through your thoughts, smile, eyes and your touch.

12. **Do no rely on words to convey your feelings to others.** Without commitment, words are cheap, useless hot air, and do not mean anything. Verbal promises are easy to break without action to back them up.

13. **People watch what you do, not what you say.** And you should pay attention to what people do, rather than what they say. We do not like to hurt others feeling, so we often say things to make them feel good. Honesty with tact is always best.

## Reclaiming Yourself

1. **If you allow others to disrespect you,** or ignore your needs, and wants, they will continue to do so because you allow it.

2. **You must acknowledge and accept** that you are important and therefore worthwhile.

3. **You must have standards for yourself** and your life. Let there be certain things you will not accept or tolerate.

4. **Never let guilt about past wrongs** get in the way of your belief that you are a worthwhile person.

5. **Pray daily to God** and ask his forgiveness for your wrongs.

6. **Daily: Have a list of names of persons** you ask to forgive you for your past wrongs to them.

7. **After you ask forgiveness,** do not commit the same errors.

8. **Daily: Forgive yourself** and others for misdeeds/abuse to yourself.

9. **Accept that you are not perfect** and neither is anyone else.

10. **Replace your addiction to others** and things with a strong love for God. Doing what you know is loving, just, and the will of God.

11. **Stand up for your rights.** Support yourself. Say what you will and will not accept. Be your own best friend.

12. **Others will respect your rights** when you acknowledge, and respect your rights.

13. **People treat us with the same respect** we feel we deserve.

14. **Do not blame others** if you let them violate your rights, disrespect you or ignore your wishes. You allow it by not taking a stand.

15. **Let people know when your needs are violated**. They are not mind readers.

To personalize this poem insert the word me or my where appropriate.

### THIS IS THE YEAR
Wonderful, Wonderful, fortunate you (me),
This is the year that your (my) dreams come true!
This is the year that your (   ) ship comes in;
This is the year you (   ) find Christ within.
This is the year you (   ) are glad to live;
This is the year you (   ) have much to give.
This is the year when you (   ) know the truth;
This is the year when you (   ) find new youth.
This is the year that brings happiness;
This is the year you (   ) will live to bless.
Wonderful, wonderful, fortunate you (   ),
This is the year that your (   ) dreams come true!
    – RUSSELL A. KEMP

## HEALING A SHATTERED SELF-IMAGE

1. Have you forgiven your parents, childhood caretakers, or others who had power to negatively influence your life? Write their name below.

2. What negative thoughts or attitude do you have toward your parents?

3. Are you able to forgive your family? How can you heal this relationship?

4. List ways you can learn to care and show positive emotions for your parents or caregivers.

5. State ways you can forgive yourself, or those who have hurt you.

    a. List below everyone you feel hate towards. What can you do to eliminate this feeling?

6. What parts of your self-image need improvement (self-worth positive self-regard/confidence? What will you do about it?

7. List things you can do to show love to yourself

8. Learning how to cope with feeling unloved
   Do you feel no one cares for you? God cares for you.

Write a letter to God in the space below -
**Dear God,**

 

a. Can you replace any negative feelings you have about yourself with positive feelings?

b. List things you can do to show you care about yourself.

c. Sit quietly, practice sending love arrows to yourself or others who mistreated you.

9. Self-Confidence – A feeling of being self-assured or comforted with what you say or do.
   a. Can you think of an activity or behavior of yours, where you feel self-assured?

   b. If not, what can you do to feel at ease with yourself?

c. Are your expectations too high or unrealistic for yourself? Remember there are no two people alike. God created everyone different and unique. Are you angry that you are special?

d. Do you tell yourself you must be perfect to be an o.k. person?

e. Do you like yourself?
Why?

Why not?

f. Is there someone you like better than yourself?
Why?

g. List below thoughts you hold about yourself, good or bad.

**HOW TO HEAL OLD HURTS FROM PAST RELATIONSHIPS**
Answer the following questions in the spaces below.

1. How has your relationship(s) in the past impacted your interactions with others? Are you able to see your faults?

2. Have you forgiven your parents, childhood caregivers, or others who had power to negatively influence your life? Write names of these persons.

3. What negative thoughts/attitudes do you have about your parents?

4. Things that block good feelings about yourself are to:
   Criticize yourself or others -
   Complain about yourself, your conditions, or others -
   Condemn yourself or others, a strong bias or prejudice-
   Can you change these habits? What will you do?

## How to Light the Fire Within You:

a. Give thanks to God for the air you breathe, the food you eat.
b. Say "yes, I can do this, or "let me give it a try."
c. Forgive yourself, your parents or friends for past      mistakes.
d. Give a smile to everyone you meet, including yourself.
e. Think peaceful thoughts.
f. Love God, yourself, and all humanity in that order
g. Never make another person your God. Put no one before God or yourself.
h. Never compare yourself to anyone. There will always be people greater or lesser than you

1. A distorted self-image, Do you know what part/s of your self-image needs changing? Ask yourself if the self-image you now have is helping you reach your goals, or do you need to create a new image to match the new you? What can you do about this? Be specific.

2. Do you have envy towards or resent anyone? If so, it will hinder your success in life. If your answer is yes, write the names below.

   Daily, forgive these people for the harm they did to you.

3. Forgive parents/caretaker – What can you do to forgive your parents to heal the hurts of this relationship?

4. How to cope with feeling unloved:
   Learn to love yourself and then transfer that good feeling to others, "Do to others as you would have them do to you."

1.  Your beliefs – What are your thoughts on what you will do with your life? Do you like yourself and other people?

2.  Self-Respect – Do you behave in a way that makes you feel good about you?

3.  An attitude is negative behavior or feelings. Do you have negative feelings?
    a)  Why?

    b)  Do you feel sorry for yourself?

4.  How can you change your self-image so it matches the person you want to be? What will you do?

5.  Self-Acceptance – state what you will do to appreciate yourself more.

6.  What can you do to get rid of self-defeating behaviors like pro-crastination, tardiness, or boredom?

7. What can you do to control the following feelings: jealousy, resentment, anger or envy?

**I feel jealous when I think about**

..............................................................................

..............................................................................

**I feel resentment when I think about**

..............................................................................

..............................................................................

**I feel angry when I think of**

..............................................................................

..............................................................................

**I feel envy when I think of**

..............................................................................

..............................................................................

8. **Write other thoughts or feelings you have below....**

..............................................................................

..............................................................................

# Chapter 10

## How to Develop Self-Esteem in the African American Adolescent

The goal is to instill pride in the African American youths for their rich diverse cultural heritage. These are positive attributes I have noticed in African Americans who have achieved, are achievers, and those who experienced segregation in the South and had strong conviction about their racial identity:

1. **Perseverance** = never giving up what one has set out to do, sticking to their purpose.
2. **Determination** = fixed purpose, great firmness in carrying out their purpose.
3. **Long suffering** = ability to endure in spite of obstacles, discomfort, or pain.
4. **Mental and physical ability** to cope with adversity.
5. **They were survivors**, surviving and achieving against great odds.
6. **Had a goal at an early age**, before the age of six.
7. **Being proud of their race**, and achieving as a Negro/Black person.
8. **Showing the world** that Negroes/Blacks were well rounded persons.
9. **Not letting their race down** by failing or giving a poor effort.
10. **Showing the world** that Negroes/Blacks were capable of achieving, and accomplishing great things.
11. **Tremendous self-determination.**
12. **Not letting anyone decide:** who you were or what you would become.

BLOCKS TO GOOD FEELINGS ABOUT YOURSELF AND OTHERS:
- Anger
- Jealousy

- Resentment/Envy
- Revenge
- Fear/anxiety

Sometimes teenagers experience all of the above emotions as they move from childhood to adulthood. In their quest to establish their independence from their families and still feel loved, they get involved in sexual relationships, instead of sensual relationships. What the adolescent wants to experience is their sensuality, or capacity to feel loving. They feel the need to separate from their parents; however, they still want to be loved. What often happens is that they confuse sensuality with sexuality and before long become a parent, while they are yet a child. There are many ways to get love from the opposite sex without ever having sexual intercourse.

Often times adolescent youths create problems for themselves by dating too early or by taking male/female dating relationships too seriously. They 'fall in love' with a false concept of what they think is love. Often they get too involved emotionally and sexually. Sexual intercourse is an adult activity that carries with it a commitment to be responsible for the outcome of one's behavior. This responsibility is the willingness of both the boy and girl to take care of the child that may be born from them having sexual intercourse. Sexual intercourse is an adult activity that God designed for us to procreate, to reproduce mankind. If you engage in sexual intercourse, you must be prepared to provide for the child that may be the result of your fooling around and having fun. Sex is not a play activity. It is not a recreational sport. If you choose to have sexual intercourse, you need to be man and woman enough to take care of your responsibility. Intimacy is possible in a relationship without you ever having sexual intercourse. You can enjoy the company of the opposite sex without having sexual intercourse. There are many ways young people can say I love you, or show their feeling for the opposite sex without having sexual intercourse. Here are 50 ways to make love without doing it.

**FIFTY WAYS TO MAKE LOVE WITHOUT DOING IT**

1. Tell the other person you like them.
2. Give the other a hug.
3. Help the other person feel important.
4. Let the other person know you care.
5. Do fun things together.
6. Be together and do nothing.
7. Make a list of things you like about the other.
8. Be there as a friend.
9. Share your inner most feelings.
10. Share a picnic lunch together.
11. Carry each others books from school.
12. Go to the library
13. Talk to each other
14. Trust one another.
15. Talk on the telephone.
16. Listens to hurts
17. Respect each other.
18. Do nice things for the other without being asked
19. Listen to music together.
20. Sing to the other
21. Give the other a flower
22. Make a treat for the other.
23. Make a hand made card for him/her.
24. Go to a movie
25. Find out what makes the other happy.
26. Play with a pet animal together
27. Be best friends.
28. Write a poem for each other
29. Take a walk together.
30. Sing together
31. Go to Church together
32. Make sacrifices for each other.

33. Think about each other.
34. Do homework together
35. Share a Popsicle together
36. Flirt with each other
37. Laugh at something funny together
38. Write each other letters
39. Walk from school together
40. Look at the sky together
41. Meet his/her family
42. Give the other a special smile
43. Go bike ridding
44. Put on a party together
45. Walk in the rain sharing an umbrella
46. Walk together holding hands
47. Read the Bible together
48. Pray for each other
49. Write nice notes to each other
50. Give each other special names

You will be able to raise self-esteem in yourself, and those around you through positive self-empowerment. To help the African American youth behave, and respond in an empowered way, have them identify the words they use when interacting with others; are they positive or negative? This will help them monitor their inner self-talk and outer behavior. The goal is to empower themselves. We must avoid the use of words or tasks that belittle or rob us of energy, drive, and vitality. When you learn how to state and set a goal for yourself for six months it enhances your feelings of self-worth.

Teach them how to monitor their inner self-talk, to change or modify their behavior by writing their thoughts on a sheet of paper, or noticing them. So they see and experience themselves different, and see others differently. Because people mirror back to us what we say, do, and who we are.

**Our good feelings (fire within us) manifest as:**

**Goal→ Drive to Excel→ Energy/Vitality→ Enthusiasm→
Aliveness Light→ = Joy, Happiness and Love**

1.  Through our desires and goals we are motivated to change.
    *   Identify or describe what motivates you to face each day?

    *   Do you have a desire to better your circumstances or life?

2.  What can you do to feel good about yourself?
    a)

    b)

3.  Do you love to please or satisfy your friends, have you made a God
    of another human like yourself?
    List things you can do to like yourself, or enjoy life more:
    a)

    b)

    c)

## If I Ruled the World

### Let's Dream

If you could have anything you wanted, live anyplace you wanted or be anything/one you wanted, what would you ask for?

**Answer these questions**

1. What famous person/s you would like to be and why?

2. In which period of time, past or future, would you choose to live, and why?

3. What foreign country/ies would you most like to visit, and why?

4. What skill/talent would you like to possess, and why?

5. What place/s in the United States would you like to visit, and why?

6. In which sport would you like to be a star, and why?

7. What kind of car would you like to own, and why?

8. For what would you like to become famous, and why?

9. Where would you most like to live, and why?

10. What would you do with a million dollars?

11. What one change would you make if you were to become President of the United States?

12. What would you like written on your tombstone when you die?

### MERGING THE PAINFUL PAST OF AFRICAN AMERICAN YOUTH
### WITH THE GLORIOUS FUTURE

African Americans have paid a great price spiritually to integrate into the larger society, to have freedom of body, economic freedom, and freedom from social isolation. To gain these freedoms, they lost the freedom of their soul. They have become more worldly and enslaved to drugs, gangs, violence, crime, indifference to each other, loss of compassion, enslavement to television, increased self-hatred, love of jewelry, and idol worship (sports people, entertainers, Hollywood actors), sexual/moral decay, and lack of a set of principles to guide our life as to what is right or wrong.

We used to pray daily for our enemy, forgive those who mistreated us, and we had faith that Jesus would see us through any challenge. In Florida and Alabama where I experienced childhood, we lived in a village setting. Everyone knew that it took a whole village to raise a child. Everyone was our mother and father. And everyone told me what to do; they told me what was right, and what was wrong. Any adult could tell me what to do; I listened and obeyed. I respected adults because (in my mother's words, "they cared enough about my welfare to speak to me when they thought I was doing something wrong," and she appreciated it. If I "disrespected" any adult by talking back to them (sassing them), I heard about it from my six-feet-tall grandmother, (who always reminded us, she was a Watusi African and not to be messed with) and my mom. And if the disrespect was considered serious, I was punished (chastised.) I can say today that every chastisement I got did me some good. It has not damaged my character, my body or my soul. I am a better person because of the chastisement I got. I was always fighting with my male cousin, who wanted to tell me what to do so I got mad and started fighting. I was headstrong and stubborn. It was wrong for me to physically fight my cousin. Every chastisement I received as a child has added to my character, to make me the sensitive, caring person I am today. I am concerned not only about my welfare, but concerned about the welfare of my African American brothers and sisters. I grew up in an African village in Pensacola, Florida. My grandmother always said that it took a whole village to raise a child. I did not understand what she meant then, but I do understand the concept today. This is why I continually act as If I am the mother of all young people. When I see them doing something wrong, I speak to them about it. And I have never been cursed at, by any child or any African American parent for disciplining their child. I guess they are as grateful as my mom, when we were disciplined in her absence. Everyone treated us as their children for they saw themselves as the mother of us all. I have two surrogate mothers that I dedicate this poem to, Cousin Betty and Cousin Ella B.

### THE MOTHER OF THEM ALL

You care about children,
Whoever they are,
Wherever they are.
They are your family members.
They are your extended family.
They are the children you see.
They are the people you pass on the streets.
They are the people you meet in the grocery store.
You give them love through your eyes,
Your smile, and your words.

You could be called a people person,
For you truly love people.
You give hope to the faint of heart.
And encouragement to the bold and brave.
You see the potential in their hearts
And you nourish that little flicker.
They sometimes call you a busy body; and
Say you put your nose into others business.
But one fact no one can deny,
Is that you care deeply for them all.
Because you see yourself,
As the mother of them all.

– IDA GREENE

## CHANGING YOUR WORLD

Make some notes about each of the following questions and be ready
to discuss your responses with your parents or teacher.

1. If you could change one thing in the world, what would it be?

2. How would this change your world, and what would the world be
   like then?

When we were segregated in the south we practiced our ancient
African family traditions of shared child rearing. Because they knew it
took a whole village to raise a child. We must move forward by taking
our rich heritage, and legacy of love for our neighbor with us. Hate is
not an option for African Americans. We must still do unto others as
we would have them do to us. We must still turn the other cheek (by
walking away from anyone, who engages us into violence); we must for-

give seventy times seven, for this is soul work. It is for our soul's salvation, not the other person, for we will return to our true Mother/Father, when we leave this planet. To the many African American children who have lost their mother and father to drugs or dysfunctional behavior, I say to you "take heart." Your mom and dad may have abandoned you, but your race will never abandon you. In the South, we said, "Some people take in stray animal, in our race we take in stray people". We have always cared about the people who were ignored or forgotten. And we care for and about our African American children, the leaders of tomorrow.

## THE AFRICAN AMERICAN PLEDGE OF ALLEGIANCE
### FOR HIGH SELF-ESTEEM

I know who I am,
I am a child of GOD.
My race is beautiful and,
My skin color is beautiful.
God has placed no limitations,
On my potential and neither do I.
– IDA GREENE

Your self-esteem is endless, it will need to be modified and corrected as you change. It is the vehicle that will take you through life. Like a car, it will need continuous maintenance. As an African American, ask yourself if your self-esteem is a Volkswagen or Mercedes Benz? Become excited about the unique, creative, genius inside you waiting to burst forth.

Anyone who genuinely wants to improve self-esteem in the African American child, needs to unconditionally accept them and love them as they are (anger, defiance, sharp tongue), and be patient as they learn to trust you inch by inch. Sometimes the process is slow, but it is worth it, and they are worth it.

## My Self

I have to live with myself, and so
    I want to be fit for myself to know,
I want to be able, as days go by,
    Always to look myself straight in the eye;
I don't want to stand, with the setting sun,
    And hate myself for the things I've done.
I don't want to keep on a closet shelf,
    A lot of secrets about myself.
And fool myself, as I come and go,
    Into thinking that nobody else will know
The kind of person that I really am;
    I don't want to dress up myself in sham.
I want to go out with my head erect,
    I want to deserve all men's respect;
But here in the struggle for fame and self,
    I want to be able to like myself.
I don't want to look at myself and know
    That I'm bluster and bluff and empty show,
I never can hide myself from me;
    I see what others may never see;
I know what others may never know;
    I never can fool myself, and so,
Whatever happens, I want to be
    Self-respecting and conscience free.
                – EDGAR A. GUEST

## My Self

I have to live with myself, and so
    I want to be fit for myself to know,
I want to be able, as days go by,
    Always to look myself straight in the eye;
I don't want to stand, with the setting sun,
    And hate myself for the things I've done.
I don't want to keep on a closet shelf,
    A lot of secrets about myself.
And fool myself, as I come and go,
    Into thinking that nobody else will know
The kind of person that I really am;
    I don't want to dress up myself in sham.
I want to go out with my head erect,
    I want to deserve all men's respect;
But here in the struggle for fame and self,
    I want to be able to like myself.
I don't want to look at myself and know
    That I'm bluster and bluff and empty show,
I never can hide myself from me;
    I see what others may never see;
I know what others may never know;
    I never can fool myself, and so,
Whatever happens, I want to be
    Self-respecting and conscience free.
                – EDGAR A. GUEST

## How to Improve Self-Esteem
## in the African American Child

Self-esteem is not a privilege. It is a right. African American children struggle daily to maintain their cultural identity, or sense of self. This book helps you understand the unique cultural underpinnings of the African American child, and how to use it to help them feel competent, so they achieve, and excel.

**Here is what others have to say about the book:**
*Remarkably Impressive. These books are a must for the Black family especially because they empower you to strive for greatness, void of fear and setbacks — A must for the American family, especially the chapter that focuses on conquering and controlling anger.*
– CAROL JOHNSON, ENTERTAINER/ENTREPRENEUR
West Hollywood, CA

*This very positive volume, with its spiritual focus, encourages us to be our very best. Greene's text and activities will help you improve your own self-esteem and that of your children.*
– ALVIN F. POUSSAINT, MD, Cambridge, MA

*Great book, offers hints for all students, and self-healing for the African American child.*
– LINA LOPEZ-DELUTE, Mentor Teacher

*A book of worth for all African Americans in building a healthy self-image.*
– CARROLL W. WAYMON, Psychologist/Educator

# Bibliography

Armstrong, Thomas. *7 Kinds of Smart*. Penguin Books USA Inc., 375 Hudson Street, New York, New York 10014, USA

*Ebony* Magazine, January 1992. Johnson Publishing Company, Inc., 820 South Michigan Avenue, Chicago, Illinois 60605

Harambee/Just Us Books, Inc., 301 Maine Street, Suite 22-24, Orange, NJ 07050.

www.ingramcontent.com/pod-product-compliance
Lightning Source LLC
Chambersburg PA
CBHW031843090426
42741CB00005B/334